D1522432

Spectacular Space Travelers

PROFILES

Amazing Archaeologists and Their Finds
America's Most Influential First Ladies
America's Third-Party Presidential Candidates
Black Abolitionists and Freedom Fighters
Black Civil Rights Champions
Charismatic Cult Leaders
Courageous Crimefighters
Environmental Pioneers
Great Auto Makers and Their Cars
Great Justices of the Supreme Court
Hatemongers and Demagogues
Hoaxers and Hustlers
Influential Economists
International Terrorists
Journalists Who Made History
Legendary Labor Leaders
Philanthropists and Their Legacies
Soviet Leaders from Lenin to Gorbachev
Spectacular Space Travelers
Top Entrepreneurs and Their Businesses
Top Lawyers and Their Famous Cases
Treacherous Traitors
Utopian Visionaries
Women Business Leaders
Women Chosen for Public Office
Women in Medicine
Women Inventors and Their Discoveries
Women of Adventure
Women of the U.S. Congress
Women Who Led Nations
Women Who Reformed Politics
Women With Wings
The World's Greatest Explorers

Spectacular
Space
Travelers

Jason Richie

The Oliver Press, Inc.
Minneapolis

THE AUTHOR WOULD LIKE TO THANK Russian space historian Aleksandr Zheleznyakov, St. Petersburg, Russia. The chapter on Alexei Leonov could not have been written without him. Thanks also to space historian William A. Larsen, Lyndon B. Johnson Space Center, for his reading of the manuscript. Mr. Larsen's vast knowledge of astronauts and the space program were a great help. Of course, any errors that remain are the author's alone. —*Jason Richie*

The Oliver Press, Inc.
Charlotte Square
5707 West 36th Street
Minneapolis, MN 55416-2510

Library of Congress Cataloging-in-Publication Data
Richie, Jason, 1966-
Spectacular Space Travelers / Jason Richie
p. cm. — (Profiles)
Includes bibliographical references and index.
    Summary: Profiles three Soviet cosmonauts and four American astronauts who accomplished "firsts" for their nations: Yuri Gagarin, Valentina Tereshkova, Alexei Leonov, Wally Schirra, Neil Armstrong, John Young, and Eileen Collins.

ISBN 1-881508-71-4 (library binding)
1. Astronauts—Biography—Juvenile literature. 2. World records—Juvenile literature. [1. Astronauts. 2. World records.] I. Title. II. Profiles (Minneapolis, Minn.)

TL789.85.A1 R53 2001
629.45'0092'2—dc21
[B]   00-052857
                                           CIP
                                           AC

ISBN 1-881508-71-4
Printed in the United States of America
07 06 05 04 03 02 01   8 7 6 5 4 3 2 1

Contents

Robert Goddard and his first rocket. This rocket wasn't much by today's standards, weighing only 16 pounds, more than 10 of which were fuel, but it launched a new era of human achievement.

Introduction

*Y*ou wouldn't have known he'd just made history by the terseness of the report. "After about 20 sec," it began,

> the rocket rose without perceptible jar, with no smoke and with no apparent increase in the rather small flame, increased rapidly in speed, and after describing a semicircle, landed 184 ft from the starting point . . . The average speed, from the time of the flight measured by a stopwatch, was 60 miles an hour.

Only the last sentence revealed the significance of the event: "It was the first time that a rocket operated by liquid propellants traveled under its own power." So went American physicist Robert Goddard's description of the first flight of a liquid-fuel rocket. It was March 16, 1926.

Goddard launched more than a rocket from his aunt's Massachusetts farm that day. Although hardly anybody except Goddard and a few other innovators realized it, liquid-fuel rockets were the key that would free humanity from its earthly shackles.

Rockets had been around for upwards of 1,000 years, originating as an astonishing technological innovation by the early Chinese. But their rockets—indeed, all rockets right up to Goddard's day—had been fueled by explosive powders (like gunpowder). Basically, these were little more than fireworks. Their performance was erratic. And they just weren't powerful enough to launch people into space.

Rockets with liquid-fuel engines were different. The flow of fuel could be controlled: therefore, the thrust of the rocket could be, too. Liquid-propellant engines could be shut off and restarted. In theory, their range was mathematically unlimited—Goddard believed they could reach the Moon or beyond.

Other innovators repeated, then surpassed, the American's success. In Germany, Johannes Winkler achieved Europe's first liquid-propellant rocket flight in March 1931. Wernher von Braun, another German rocket pioneer, was 19 years old at the time of Winkler's breakthrough. Over the next dozen years, von Braun spearheaded development of the world's first ballistic missile—the liquid-fuel V-2. Although the V-2 was a military weapon that showered destruction on Nazi Germany's

8

The U.S. Army brought a team of German rocket scientists to the United States after World War II. Headed by Major General Holger Toftoy (standing left) the group included (left to right) Ernst Stuhlinger, Hermann Oberth, Wernher von Braun, and Robert Lusser.

enemies during the last months of World War II, it wasn't the missile's military application that motivated von Braun. He desperately wanted to build rockets capable of space travel. In May 1945, von Braun was captured by Allied forces just before the war ended in Germany's defeat. He willingly moved to the United States, where he continued his quest to reach space by working in America's infant rocket program.

Meanwhile, in the Soviet Union, Sergei Korolev was crafting his own space rockets. He was in his mid-20s when he helped design Russia's first liquid-fuel rocket. When it raced skyward in March 1933, Korolev left no doubt as to his ultimate goal: "Soviet rockets must conquer space!" he insisted. After the war he gained control of the Soviet missile program and attempted to do just that.

Sergei Korolev (far left) and members of GIRD (Group for the Study of Jet Propulsion) posed in 1933 with their GIRD-X rocket in a forest near Moscow.

A race was on. But it wasn't a space race, not at first anyway. In the late 1940s and early 1950s, von Braun and Korolev competed to develop the first intercontinental ballistic missiles. They had no choice. Their governments demanded rockets armed with atomic warheads, not rockets designed to carry scientific equipment or people into space. Only when it became clear in the mid-1950s that a race to explore space could also benefit national security did government leaders permit their rocket scientists to shoot for the stars, too.

Soviet leader Nikita Khrushchev came to realize that a steady stream of space "spectaculars" could humiliate the United States in front of the rest of the world— especially developing nations not yet aligned with either superpower. Khrushchev hoped that such upstaging would convince the less powerful countries that Soviet global dominance was inevitable and that they had better start lining up on the winning side. That was Khrushchev's goal in allowing Korolev to launch *Sputnik 1*—the world's first artificial satellite—in October 1957. Rocket and satellite worked as intended and the world had to admit that, yes, Soviet engineering and technical know-how seemed to have outpaced America's. That success only whetted Khrushchev's appetite for more.

America and the rest of the western world were frightened by this initial defeat in the space race. Any missile capable of throwing a satellite into orbit around

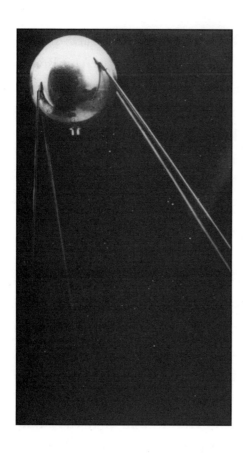

The first Sputnik, which means satellite in Russian, was 23 inches in diameter and weighed 184 pounds. Transmitting a "beep-beep" signal, Sputnik 1 *orbited Earth for 21 days before it reentered the atmosphere and burned. The Soviets later launched* Sputnik 2 *and* 3.

Earth could, in theory, drop a nuclear bomb anywhere along the way. "Clearly they have established a great lead in missile technology," editorialized one British newspaper. President Dwight Eisenhower of the United States had purposely avoided entering a costly race to put a satellite in orbit. But now he admitted that *Sputnik 1*'s success had "precipitated a wave of apprehension throughout the Free World" that forced the United States to take "added efforts" to reaffirm its technological and military superiority.

One such effort was the creation of the National Aeronautics and Space Administration, or NASA, on October 1, 1958. In the carefree, pre-Sputnik era, research into high-speed and high-altitude flight had been divided among several independent civilian and military organizations. The new NASA absorbed the civilian groups and took over much of the military's work. With a rising fear of more humiliations from the Soviets, America committed itself to winning the next heat in the space race. And everyone knew where the finish line lay. It was NASA's primary reason for being—to launch the first piloted spacecraft.

In the U.S. and the Soviet Union, the first space travelers would be military pilots. Space officials from both nations believed that although the first capsules would not require complex piloting, experienced flyers would handle the physical and emotional stresses of space flight (like weightlessness and isolation) better than non-pilots. In the United States, there was Eisenhower's added edict that all astronauts be test pilots—elite flyers who routinely risked their lives (and still do) testing experimental and newly delivered production aircraft.

From among 324 candidates, the Americans picked seven finalists in April 1959. One of their number would lift off in a cone-shaped, single-seat Mercury capsule. The initial group of 20 Soviet space travelers, who were called cosmonauts, were chosen in March 1960 from perhaps 200 or more applicants. Because of strict weight

The seven Mercury Astronauts posed with a model of the booster rocket and Mercury capsule they all hoped to hitch a ride on. Seated, left to right: Virgil Grissom, Malcolm Scott Carpenter, Donald K. Slayton, and Leroy Gordon Cooper Jr. Standing, left to right: Alan B. Shepard Jr., Walter Marty Schirra Jr., and John H. Glenn Jr.

and height limits, only six trained for the historic first flight aboard the ball-shaped, one-person Vostok. Which nation would win this contest? Which pilot would live forever in the history books as the first human in space?

The answers are the Soviet Union and cosmonaut Yuri Gagarin. On April 12, 1961, *Vostok 1* carried Gagarin around the world in less than two hours. His triumph shocked and angered the American people all over again. When astronaut Alan Shepard roared into space atop a von Braun-designed rocket three weeks later, he was hailed as a hero upon his return. Although his 15-minute flight was only a suborbital "hop" (up into space and back down to earth without orbiting) designed to test the Mercury spacecraft, Americans were elated to have finally fielded their own runner.

Emboldened by Shepard's success, President John Kennedy determined to beat the Soviets once and for all. On May 25, 1961, he drew a third and final finish line in the race for space—right across the surface of the Moon. It was a bold move for the youthful president; an American hadn't even orbited Earth yet. (John Glenn would make that flight in February 1962.) A Moon mission would require complex skills, techniques, and equipment yet to be developed. Astronauts would need to learn to rendezvous and dock two spacecraft in orbit, because one ship alone would never be enough to complete a trip to the Moon. They had to be able to live in space for up to two weeks, the time needed for a thorough lunar exploration. And they had to be able to leave the safety of their spacecraft to walk on the Moon. Could the astronauts do all this by the end of the decade, as Kennedy stipulated?

The Soviets, of course, believed they would win the race to the Moon. In August 1962, two orbiting Vostok capsules passed within four miles of each other. They didn't rendezvous—that is, fly in close formation—but the Russians appeared to be taking the first steps. Ten months later, *Vostok 6* carrying Valentina Tereshkova, the first woman in space, closed to within three miles of a companion craft. The joining of two Soviet spacecraft in orbit seemed imminent. Then came the first space walk by Alexei Leonov in March 1965. Chalk up another "first" for the Soviet Union.

Leonov's leap turned out to be the high point of the Soviet Moon program. America's overwhelming strength has long rested on its ability and willingness to mobilize

U.S. President John F. Kennedy (left) and Soviet Premier Nikita Khrushchev extended the nuclear arms race between their countries to include a dash for technological supremacy in space.

great resources in times of war. And this was a war, even if just a "cold" one. NASA had enough funding and talented personnel to build better rockets, spacecraft, and the launch facilities to support them. Given such advantages, American astronauts took the lead in the Moon race for good in 1965. Walter "Wally" Schirra piloted the first rendezvous in December. Neil Armstrong performed the first docking in March 1966. Others walked in space and set records for mission longevity. In May 1969, two astronauts even flew a lunar landing craft to within nine miles of the Moon. By then, the exhausted Soviets had fallen out of the race. It took only Armstrong's epic "small step" on the lunar surface two months later to complete America's come-from-behind victory.

With the Moon race behind them, the two space programs went their separate ways. The Soviets launched the first space station in 1971. Over the next two decades, they perfected the ability to live and work for extended periods in space. The Americans, meanwhile, developed the first reusable spacecraft—an orbiter to "shuttle" astronauts and equipment to and from space. John Young, making a record fifth space flight, commanded the first space shuttle mission in April 1981.

Astronauts and cosmonauts had achieved many spectacular feats by the early 1980s. They had walked in space, joined their capsules in orbit, and walked on the Moon. They had lived aboard space stations for months at a time and had flown reusable space planes to precise runway landings. There was, however, one shortcoming on the otherwise impressive list of accomplishments—it included only one woman's name.

Many thought Valentina Tereshkova's flight in 1963 should have opened the door for other female space travelers. That didn't happen. Tales of a poor performance dogged Tereshkova for years. None of this has been confirmed, but the uncertainty did nothing to help the case of women in either space program.

A second woman finally flew in 1982—Svetlana Savitskaya of the Soviet Union. Then, Sally Ride of the United States orbited a year later. In July 1984, Savitskaya returned to orbit to walk in space. She was followed by

Svetlana Savitskaya visited the Salyut 7 *space station on both of her historic missions. An aeronautical engineer, Savitskaya was also an aerobatics pilot and master parachutist before joining the Soviet space program in 1980.*

American Kathryn Sullivan, who walked out of the space shuttle in October. Women were on the move, that was certain, but a woman still hadn't piloted a spacecraft. Nor had a woman commanded a mission. (All the early Vostoks were automatic. Like Gagarin before her, Tereshkova neither piloted nor commanded her craft.) Both these "firsts" would fall to the same woman. Astronaut Eileen Collins, a former test pilot in the U.S. Air Force, piloted shuttle flights in 1995 and 1997, then commanded a mission in 1999.

Collins closed more than just a gender gap in space. As the Soviets built space stations after 1970, they found themselves unable to afford reusable ground-to-orbit transports. For the Americans, the problem was just the opposite. They had the shuttles, but other than the short-lived *Skylab* space station in 1973-1974, no permanent orbital outpost to service.

This began to change on Collins's first space flight in 1995. She piloted a rendezvous with the Russian station *Mir*, a dress rehearsal for an actual docking performed by a later shuttle crew. Within a few years, cosmonauts routinely joined shuttle missions, while Americans sometimes spent months on the Russian space station. Cooperation between the two nations continued with con-struction of the International Space Station beginning in 1998. Indeed, shuttle flights to and from the new orbital outpost, *Alpha*, typically include crew members from many nations. The space race is over for good. Everyone won.

Yuri Alexeyevich Gagarin (1934-1968) earned a place in history—and in the hearts of people everywhere—when he became the first person to leave Earth and travel through space.

1

Yuri Gagarin
"Here we go!"

*I*t was early morning, April 12, 1961. At the foot of the big multistage rocket was an elevator. There the small man in the orange space suit turned to face the engineers and technicians gathered to see him off. "The whole of my life seems to be condensed into one wonderful moment," he told the crowd. "In all times and epochs the greatest happiness for man has been to take part in new discoveries. To be the first to enter the cosmos, to engage, single-handed, in an unprecedented duel with nature— could one dream of anything more?" The cosmonaut

From the top of the steps, Gagarin gave the ground crew a final wave on April 12 before entering the elevator that lifted him up to the waiting Vostok 1.

raised both hands skyward in a salute, then disappeared into the elevator.

Once strapped into the capsule's ejection seat, Yuri Gagarin had to wait a few hours until launch. There was the clank of wrenches as technicians sealed the hatch, then more clanking as they reopened the hatch to check a faulty sensor. Gagarin closed his eyes and tried to relax.

The soft music ground controllers piped into the cabin helped. Then came the call: "T minus 15 minutes!" Gagarin slipped into his gloves and snapped his helmet's visor down. A knock from somewhere told him the lift tower was being removed. "T minus 5 minutes!" Time moved quickly now. At 60 seconds, he shifted his weight and grasped the ejection handle tightly in both hands.

It started quietly at first, a faint rumble barely audible to the man perched high above the rocket's main engines. As the fiery blast of ignition exploded up and out, however, the unmistakable sensation of upward movement suddenly gripped Gagarin. *Vostok 1* was climbing! Over the roar of the engines, now almost deafening, came the cosmonaut's excited shout: "Here we go!"

Yuri Alexeyevich Gagarin was born on March 9, 1934, in the village of Klushino, Russia. Klushino, about 75 miles west of Moscow, was a collective farm where all families shared the work and the food they produced. When Yuri was born, Alexei and Anna Gagarin had a 10-year-old son, Valentin, and a 7-year-old daughter, Zoya. A fourth child, Boris, was born after Yuri.

Poverty gripped everyone in Klushino. Nevertheless, Yuri and his siblings were happy. The boys often helped their father, who was one of the collective's carpenters. When the children weren't working, they swam and fished and played ball in the village fields. Yuri especially liked sleeping outside with Uncle Pavel Gagarin, gazing at the stars and dreaming of life on other worlds.

In June 1941, the Germans invaded the Soviet Union, the start of four bloody years for Yuri's country during World War II. Remarkably, none in his family were among the 20 million Russians who lost their lives. The Gagarins did lose their home, however, to the German troops occupying the area. Alexei built an underground bunker where his family lived, protected from the artillery and aircraft. It was February 1943 before the battered German forces retreated. A little over two years later, on May 7, 1945, the war in Europe ended.

Yuri's family moved closer to Moscow after the war, to a town called Gzhatsk. There, the boy finally started formal schooling. During the war, he had developed a fascination with the airplanes he saw. One Soviet pilot had even shown Yuri the inside of his plane. Now Yuri met another flyer, a former pilot named Lev Bespalov who taught sixth-grade science. Bespalov helped Yuri build a model airplane and predicted that the excited boy would one day fly the real thing.

In 1949, Yuri left school and set out on his own to Moscow. In the Soviet Union at the time, formal schooling ended after the seventh grade. Impatient to get on with his life, Yuri quit a year early. He wanted to be a locomotive engineer but found work instead as an apprentice in a foundry (a type of factory where metals are cast into tools). The job was hard and the hours long, but it was thrilling nonetheless for a young man who couldn't wait to be on his own.

Two years later, Yuri entered the Saratov Industrial Technical School (about 500 miles southeast of Moscow) to study factory management. There, he met yet another influential science teacher, Nikolai Moskvin. Moskvin assigned Yuri to write a paper on the work of Konstantin Tsiolkovsky. In a remarkable series of articles written between 1883 and 1935, Tsiolkovsky had developed all the major principles that would one day govern space flight. He was the first to theorize about liquid-fuel rockets, orbiting space stations, devices for spacecraft guidance, and the use of pressurized suits to work in space. Tsiolkovsky even predicted that by the early 1960s a person would travel to space aboard a multistage rocket! To

Russian teacher Konstantin Eduardovich Tsiolkovsky (1857-1935) envisioned using rockets to explore space.

Yuri Gagarin, captivated by flight since childhood, the idea of space travel was almost too exciting to consider.

Deciding to do something about his obsession with aircraft, Gagarin took flying lessons at the Saratov Flying Club. But before he was allowed to pilot a plane, he had to learn to parachute from one. Gagarin's first jump nearly became his last when his main chute failed to open. Only his calm reliance on the backup saved his life. Finally, in the summer of 1955, Gagarin flew. From that moment, he knew it would be the way he'd spend the rest of his life.

"The rest of his life" began a little sooner than he expected. In late 1955, Gagarin was drafted into the Soviet Air Force. His flying experience landed him in the military flight school at Orenburg (about 350 miles east of Saratov), where he trained on the Soviet Union's premier combat jet, the MIG. Yuri fell in love with the aircraft immediately—except for one small problem. At five feet, two inches tall, he had to sit on a cushion to see well enough to land the plane.

Gagarin graduated on November 7, 1957. The same day he married Valentina Goryacheva, whom he had met at a dance the previous year. They honeymooned, then left for Lieutenant Gagarin's first duty station.

Although Gagarin now was flying exactly what he wanted, he wasn't satisfied. *Sputnik 1* and *Sputnik 2*, the world's first artificial satellites, had been blasted into orbit from the Soviet Union during Gagarin's last two months in flight school. In May 1958, the Soviets launched a third satellite. These were followed by *Luna 1* in January 1959. It missed the Moon, but *Luna 2* and *Luna 3*, launched in September and October 1959, were monumental achievements for the Soviets. *Luna 2* struck the Moon and *Luna 3* snapped the first photographs of its dark side. For Gagarin, merely streaking through the atmosphere no longer seemed challenging. He wanted to fly through space and applied for cosmonaut training.

Five months of intense physical and psychological examinations followed. The Soviet doctors demanded perfect health, physically and mentally. From hundreds of air force volunteers, 20 were chosen in March 1960 as the first cosmonauts. Yuri Gagarin was one.

Serious training now began at Zvezdograd ("Star City"), the cosmonaut training center outside Moscow. To the parachute jumping and coordination drills of the selection phase were added more demanding tasks. The centrifuge whipped the cosmonauts around as though at the end of a long rope. This conditioned them to the increased forces of gravity (g-forces, or g's) they would feel during the acceleration of launch and deceleration of atmospheric reentry.

Training on the centrifuge, the cosmonauts had to endure forces up to 10 times (10 g's) the normal gravity of Earth, which required special breathing techniques just to remain conscious. But the centrifuge was easy compared to the "iron maiden." This infamous device spun the

Essentially an aircraft seat attached to the end of a long metal arm, the centrifuge was used to accustom Soviet cosmonauts to the physical discomfort they would feel during launch and reentry.

nauseated cosmonauts around three axes at once—forwards, sideways, and around and around like a top. And this ride was made in total darkness!

The final phase of training involved flying simulated missions in spacecraft mockups. Everything about the capsule was reproduced—the pilot's flight controls, the radio communication system, the environmental control system, and more. Of course, if all went as planned, the cosmonauts would not have to do any flying; Soviet spacecraft were meant to operate automatically.

Sadly, the reasons for this design had nothing to do with safety of the cosmonauts or engineering requirements. For one thing, government officials feared the cosmonauts might pass out from g-forces or weightlessness and crash. Not only would this embarrass the Soviet government, but also there was the unthinkable possibility that the out-of-control capsule would land in "enemy" territory—that is to say, any territory not controlled by the Soviet Union. Then there was the worry that cosmonauts with too much control might defect (leave their country) from space by purposely landing outside the Soviet Union.

In the end, a compromise solution was settled upon: the Soviet capsules were given manual controls in case the automatic systems failed, but they could only be activated by first inputting a code that only ground controllers knew. In other words, that information had to be radioed up to the cosmonaut in an emergency. But what if the radio failed? Sergei Korolev, the chief designer, worked around this restriction by secretly taping an envelope containing the code inside the spacecraft. This would certainly have been considered treason by government officials.

The Soviet capsules, which were named Vostok, had two separate parts: a sphere housing the cosmonaut and a cone-shaped service module containing the spacecraft's guidance, fuel, and propulsion systems. The sphere measured about seven and a half feet across, with the attached service module stretching another eight and a half feet to the rear. Minus the cosmonaut, Vostok craft weighed approximately 10,400 pounds at launch. (A present-day mid-size automobile would make a good length comparison, although a Vostok would be about twice as heavy.) Finally, a rocket weighing half a million pounds and standing as tall as a 12-story building would blast the combined craft 185 miles into space.

For the first flight, Soviet space leader Sergei Korolev eventually narrowed the pool of cosmonauts to six. On April 8, 1961, he made his choice. Yuri Gagarin would launch in four days.

April 12 dawned early for Gagarin. He woke at 5:30 A.M., ate a breakfast of meat paste and blackberry jam, then was helped into his pressure suit and bright orange coveralls. (The bold color was meant to help recovery crews spot the cosmonaut once he parachuted out of the craft after returning from orbit.) A short bus ride to the launch site followed. Shortly after 7:00 A.M., Gagarin slid through the hatch of *Vostok 1*. At 9:07, the booster rocket's 20 engines fired. As the mounting g's pressed Gagarin into his seat, *Vostok 1* climbed faster and faster into the eastern sky. The first-stage engines burned out and fell away, then the second stage, and finally the third. Fourteen minutes had now passed and *Vostok 1*

Sergei Pavlovich Korolev (1907-1966, left) and the man he chose to ride his spacecraft, Yuri Gagarin. Known only by his title, chief designer, Korolev's identity was kept a state secret until after his death.

was traveling at 17,500 mph, orbiting through the upper fringes of Earth's atmosphere at an altitude of more than 106 miles.

During this time, only the spacecraft's speed kept it from reentering the lower atmosphere. This speed balanced the gravitational pull of Earth. Imagine a ball

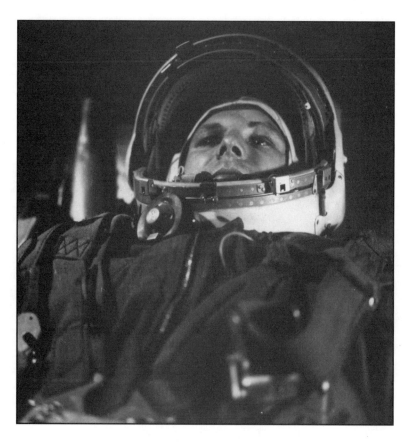

Yuri Gagarin seated inside Vostok 1

swung around on the end of a string. The inward pull of the string balances the outward centrifugal force of the ball. To reach a higher orbit, *Vostok 1* would have to increase speed. To slow down and drop from orbit, *Vostok 1's* retrorocket would have to fire and slow the spacecraft down.

Gagarin later recalled the exceptional blackness above *Vostok 1* and how it magnified the clarity and brightness of the stars. Looking earthward, he "could easily make out the continents, islands, big rivers, large reservoirs, [and] land faults." The sensation of weightlessness posed no problem. As a jet pilot, Gagarin had experienced the feeling during certain aerial maneuvers. He ate and drank with no difficulty. Writing proved trickier. When he opened his tablet to write a report, his pencil floated away. He could only chuckle as he slipped the paper back into his pocket.

Everything was going smoothly at 10:25 A.M. when *Vostok 1*'s retrorocket fired. Following a 40-second burn, the service module was designed to separate from the capsule. *Vostok 1* would then fall through the atmosphere like a flaming meteor, its occupant protected from the 3,000° F heat of reentry by the sphere's protective coating. Unfortunately, Gagarin's deorbit didn't quite work as it was supposed to. Separation of the service module never occurred. The capsule burned through the atmosphere trailing the module by a few unsevered cables, causing both to tumble wildly. "There was a moment," Gagarin later recalled, when "everything seemed to go gray." Fortunately, the searing heat eventually melted the cables, releasing the service module.

As *Vostok 1* fell through 23,000 feet above Earth, its cosmonaut experienced the end of his thrill ride. Just behind his head, explosives blew the hatch off. Two seconds later, twin rockets at the base of Gagarin's ejection seat blasted him through the opening. This time his parachute opened. Gagarin landed just outside Saratov, the site of his first jump six years earlier. As he walked toward the town, he saw a mother and child approaching him. One look at the strange creature in the orange space suit stopped them dead in their tracks. "I am one of yours, a Soviet," Gagarin reassured them. "I've come from outer space."

Humanity's first leap into the cosmos lasted 108 minutes. In that span of time, Yuri Gagarin's life changed forever. Even before he landed, Soviet officials had promoted him two ranks from lieutenant to major. Then, of course, there was the small matter of worldwide fame that greeted his return. Gagarin was honored with a massive parade in Moscow, met with the highest Soviet leaders, and visited several European capitals.

The following month, Gagarin was named chief cosmonaut. In that post, which he held until March 1966, he directed the training of the other cosmonauts. After December 1963, he also served as deputy director of the Cosmonaut Training Center. Besides his official duties, Gagarin attended the Zhukovsky Air Force Engineering Academy, graduating in February 1968 with a degree in aeronautical engineering.

One thing Gagarin never achieved was a second flight into space. In June 1964, Soviet officials grounded him for fear he might lose his life in space—and they a national hero. Although Gagarin won reinstatement in April 1966, the death of another cosmonaut during a

34

Two days after his flight on April 12, 1961, the people of Moscow joyously welcomed Yuri Gagarin, standing center in the car. Soviet leader Nikita Khrushchev and Gagarin's wife, Valentina, rode with him.

mission a year later temporarily suspended all space flights. On March 27, 1968, while flying to maintain his skills for the time when orbital flights resumed, Yuri Gagarin was killed when he lost control of his MIG fighter and crashed. His country honored him by placing his ashes alongside other Soviet heroes in the Kremlin Wall in Moscow's Red Square.

The first woman to venture into space, Valentina Vladimirovna Tereshkova (b. 1937) orbited Earth 48 times in 3 days during her historic trip.

2

Valentina Tereshkova
Citizen Cosmonaut

*U*ntil June 16, 1963, space travel was the exclusive domain of military pilots. Both Soviet and American space officials believed military flyers were the most suited to handle the rigors of space flight. High g-forces, brief weightlessness, and unexpected problems requiring split-second solutions were all sensations or situations elite pilots often faced.

At least two people were willing to bet their necks that civilians with little flying experience could handle orbital flight. One was Soviet premier Nikita Khrushchev.

His nation had launched *Sputnik*, the first artificial satellite, in 1957 and Yuri Gagarin, the first space traveler, in 1961. It would be an even greater propaganda victory for Khrushchev if a common Soviet worker could orbit Earth. And how much sweeter the triumph if that worker were a woman! Khrushchev could crow to the world how the communist East valued equality of the sexes more than the capitalist West.

The second person who believed that civilians could handle space flight was Valentina Tereshkova, a factory worker from a peasant family. She understood that she was precisely the type of woman Khrushchev wanted to publicize and that her flight would be little more than a publicity stunt. She didn't care. This was her chance. Propaganda or not, Tereshkova was about to ride a rocket into space. And she would be the first woman to do it!

Valentina Vladimirovna Tereshkova was born in the town of Maslennikovo, Russia, on March 6, 1937. "Valya" was the daughter of Vladimir and Yelena Tereshkova. (Her parents followed the Russian tradition that children take the father's first name as their middle name, with boys' names ending in *vich* and girls' ending in *ovna*.) About 190 miles northeast of Moscow, Maslennikovo was a collective farm where all residents shared the labor and the food they produced. There, Vladimir drove a tractor and worked as a mechanic. Father and daughter were close, and Vladimir even taught the budding tomboy to drive the tractor when she was barely four years old.

Vladimir never lived to see Valya grow up. He was killed fighting the Germans during World War II when she was six. Soviet society suffered terribly during the war. Valya and her two siblings—an older sister and younger brother—weren't the only ones to lose a father. Occasionally, some of the men did return, although usually not before being injured in the fighting. Despite their hardships, the Soviet people endured and defeated the Germans. Valya developed a fighting spirit and an immense pride in her country.

Soon after the war ended in 1945, Valya's family moved 40 miles north to the town of Yaroslavl. There she attended elementary school, then high school. Valya's craving for ever-greater adventures became readily apparent during these years. When many of her friends declined the challenge, it was Valya who swam across the Kotorosl River near her home. Then there was the time she jumped from the river's tall bridge head first, arms outstretched—a feat only the oldest boys would attempt. It was Valya's first flight. She liked the feeling.

Valya graduated from Girls High School Number 32 in spring 1953. She had hoped to study to become a locomotive engineer, but her mother was too poor to pay the tuition. Valya found work in a tire factory and went to technical school at night. She eventually learned how to repair machines used in the textile industry and began working in a cotton-fabric plant in 1960.

It was in technical school in late 1958 that Valya met Galina Shashkova. Known as "Galya" to her friends, Shashkova had an intriguing hobby—she jumped out of planes. It didn't take much for Galya to convince Valya to join the parachuting club. After six months of training, Valya made her first jump in May 1959. It was the Kotorosl bridge all over again. Valya was hooked. She jumped 126 times over the next two years.

In 1960, Tereshkova joined the Young Communist League at the textile plant where she worked. She often traveled to historic sites with the group. On one trip, she visited a space museum in Moscow and stood fascinated in front of the many displays. In one corner was a replica of *Sputnik 1*, launched into orbit in October 1957. Beside it stood a mockup of *Sputnik 2*, which blasted off a month later with the dog Laika aboard. It isn't hard to imagine the thoughts racing through the adventuresome Tereshkova's mind as she studied the satellite that had carried a living animal into space.

Yuri Gagarin's orbital mission in April 1961 affected her more deeply. Tereshkova read Gagarin's biography and learned that he, too, had been born a peasant. Gagarin had even worked in a foundry, a sort of factory, and had made parachute jumps in his spare time. When cosmonaut Gherman Titov became the second man in space in August 1961, Tereshkova did something impulsive (again!). She sat down and wrote a letter to officials in Moscow. She thought she could be a cosmonaut, too.

Gherman Stepanovich Titov (1935-2000) spent 24 hours in orbit aboard Vostok 2.

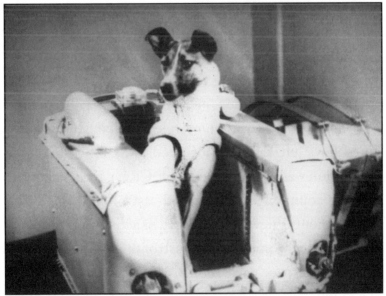

Sputnik 2 *was five times larger than its predecessor and carried a passenger: Laika ("barker" in Russian). Monitoring equipment recorded that the little dog suffered no ill effects from the launch and weightlessness, but she died a week later when her air supply ran out.*

41

Her timing couldn't have been better. Soviet leader Nikita Khrushchev was itching to one-up the United States in space again. The Sputniks had been huge victories for Soviet science and technology. In response, it seemed the United States could achieve only what the British press labeled "flopniks." (*Vanguard*, America's attempt to reach orbit, had exploded on the launch pad in December 1957. Not until the end of January 1958 was an American satellite, *Explorer I*, a reality.) The Soviet Union won again in April 1961 with Yuri Gagarin's flight aboard *Vostok 1*. Now Khrushchev wanted more. Why not put a woman into space? But not just any woman would do. Khrushchev wanted no doctors, engineers, or even pilots. He wanted a common worker. Aides selected four women from among thousands of volunteers in the wake of Gagarin's mission, including Valentina Tereshkova.

Following a series of interviews and medical exams, Tereshkova left Yaroslavl for good in March 1962. Her destination was Zvezdograd ("Star City"), the cosmonaut training complex 45 miles northeast of Moscow. The next 15 months flew by in a flurry of activity. Tereshkova and the other women learned astronomy, biology, mathematics, and space navigation. And they trained in sports like gymnastics and parachuting. In fact, in most areas they trained just like the men—with one important exception. Since none of the women knew how to fly, they weren't allowed to pilot the facility's jet trainers. The men, in contrast, had spent years flying high-performance

42

Star City, where cosmonauts still live and train for space flight

aircraft. Many had faced the terror of midflight malfunctions; some had barely escaped crashes. How the women's lack of piloting experience would affect their ability to adapt to liftoff and orbital flight was the experiment's great unknown.

The female cosmonauts did endure the usual regimen of space-flight simulations. The centrifuge, an aircraft seat attached to the end of a 50-foot-long arm,

Valentina Tereshkova training in the gym hall at Star City

whipped them around at varying speeds to simulate the increased gravity of launch and reentry into the atmosphere. Other simulators ranged from simple devices such as swinging tables and revolving chairs to complex—and nauseating—machines like the "iron maiden." Once seated inside the contraption's metal box, the cosmonauts were spun, pitched, and rolled until they managed to stop the tumbling "spacecraft" with their hand controller. To simulate weightlessness, they rode in transport airplanes that traced great arches through the sky. At the top of the arch, as Earth's gravitational pull balanced against the passenger's centrifugal (or outward) movement, the cosmonauts floated freely about the cabin. Although the sensation lasted less than 45 seconds, the maneuver could be repeated as often as needed.

In May 1963, Soviet space leader Sergei Korolev picked Tereshkova to make the first female space flight. She was set to lift off in June aboard *Vostok 6*, a spacecraft almost identical to the one Gagarin flew into space, with a spherical cabin and a cone-shaped service module.

The Soviets planned to launch Tereshkova a day after sending cosmonaut Valeri Bykovsky into space aboard *Vostok 5*. If timed right, Tereshkova's launch would place her in orbit just three miles behind her male counterpart. To foreign observers, it then would appear as though the two craft had performed a controlled rendezvous or, at the very least, had had the ability to make the attempt. Either would be a major breakthrough. Any Moon mission, which both the Soviets and Americans had by this time committed themselves to trying, would require at least two vehicles to rendezvous and dock in orbit. If Tereshkova and Bykovsky rendezvoused, the world would think the Soviets were winning the race to the Moon.

In reality, rendezvous and docking required more complex equipment and piloting techniques than either the Soviets or the Americans possessed in 1963. The world knew this about the U.S. space program because it was open to the media. The Soviet program, on the other hand, was strictly off limits. As far as anyone knew, the Vostoks could rendezvous. If nothing went terribly wrong during Tereshkova's and Bykovsky's flights, Khrushchev's deception could very well work.

Vostok 5 lifted off on June 14, followed two days later by Tereshkova in *Vostok 6*. The craft's ascent went smoothly, as did the transition to orbit a few minutes later. "Everything is fine," she radioed excitedly from an altitude of 120 miles. "I see the horizon; it's a sky blue with a dark strip. How beautiful the earth is!"

Valentina Tereshkova also saw *Vostok 5*, three miles ahead in a slightly lower orbit. That was the closest she got. Because Tereshkova had been launched into a higher orbit, it took her longer to circle Earth than Bykovsky. She steadily lost ground on *Vostok 5* as a result. Still, as Khrushchev had hoped, some American journalists concluded the Russians had actually attempted a rendezvous. And, of course, Tereshkova's participation in the event made the whole thing more spectacular. One U.S. senator even suggested that Khrushchev's citizen cosmonaut had proven "that you don't have to have 20 years of test pilot experience before you can handle one of these capsules."

46

Tereshkova used the call name "seagull" in her broadcasts back to Earth. Her family thought she had been selected for a special skydiving team and did not know Valya was a cosmonaut until she was in space.

Some accounts of what happened next suggest the senator may have spoken too soon. Official Soviet histories insist Tereshkova adapted so well to space flight that her original one-day mission was lengthened to three. This is entirely possible. Tereshkova did stay in orbit for three days. Other accounts, especially those from two former Soviet officials, suggest something different. Her flight, they insisted, was not extended from one day, but rather shortened from five days to prevent an embarrassing failure. In their versions, Tereshkova became violently space sick during the mission and had to be brought down early. Furthermore, one of the officials described Valya Tereshkova as having been "at the edge of psychological stability."

Which stories are true? It is difficult to say, since accurate information from the former Soviet Union is still hard to come by. The evidence does seem to suggest, however, that Tereshkova, without the extensive piloting experience of the other cosmonauts, could not handle the intense experience of space flight. Weightlessness could very well have caused her to suffer from space sickness. She wouldn't have been the first; cosmonaut Gherman Titov (the second Soviet in space) had become nauseated during his flight in August 1961. And Titov was considered by his comrades to be every bit as competent as Gagarin. The point is, space flight was simply an extension of what Titov and Gagarin had done for years. They knew how to push through the nausea and any other setback they might encounter. Tereshkova may not have. If she did crack, it was almost certainly because—for once—she had bitten off more than she could chew.

Vostok 6 reentered the lower atmosphere on June 19. As had Gagarin before her, Tereshkova ejected through the side hatch of the spacecraft as it dropped through 23,000 feet and floated down under her parachute. In three days, the spacecraft had traveled 48 times around

Valentina Tereshkova (right) inspecting her spacecraft

Earth—a distance greater than 1.2 million miles. That's about one-third more miles than all American astronauts combined had flown up to that time. Regardless of what had happened during her flight, the impulsive young woman from Maslennikovo had blazed a new trail to space.

Tereshkova became an instant global celebrity. Khrushchev had wisely timed her flight to coincide with the International Congress of Women being held in Moscow. There, before 2,000 women from more than 100 countries, Tereshkova was honored on June 24. "She stood firmly on her feet," Khrushchev himself said in opening remarks, "and now has risen to such heights as no person in the capitalist world brought up by wealthy daddies and mommies can rise." Trips to Cuba, Mexico, India, Eastern Europe, Africa, and Southeast Asia followed over the next several months. Tereshkova even appeared before the United Nations General Assembly in New York City. She was turning out to be as perfect a hero as Khrushchev could have hoped for.

Later that year, in November, Tereshkova married fellow cosmonaut Andrian Nikolayev. The two had one daughter, Yelena, born June 8, 1964. After the birth of her daughter, Tereshkova attended the Zhukovsky Military Air Academy. She graduated near the top of her class in 1969 with a degree in aerospace engineering.

Shortly after Tereshkova left the air academy, space officials disbanded the female cosmonaut corps. The first woman in space never made a second flight. Tereshkova served in the Supreme Soviet (the public's general assembly) from 1966 until the breakup of the Soviet Union in 1991. Along the way, she also represented her nation during the International Women's Year in Mexico City in 1975. She continues to make her home in Moscow.

Evidence surfaced in 1987 that suggested Valya Tereshkova might have been training for a second space

Valentina Tereshkova was warmly welcomed in France in 1964. Behind her, in military uniform, stands Andrian Grigoryevich Nikolayev, her husband and fellow cosmonaut. Nikolayev set endurance records on both of his flights into space.

flight, perhaps even a space walk, in the mid-1960s. That never happened, of course, but it does leave open the possibility that her historic mission in 1963 did not go so badly. Still, for many years after the flight of *Vostok 6*, a fog of uncertainty hung over the head of its cosmonaut—and, indeed, over the heads of all the women who had hoped to follow Tereshkova. It would be 19 years before a second female cosmonaut flew into space, and 36 before a woman—an American test pilot—commanded a mission. But that's another story.

Alexei Arkhipovich Leonov (b. 1934) scored another first for the Soviet Union when he walked in space in March 1965. Like most cosmonauts, Leonov was a pilot in the Soviet Air Force, as pictured here in 1956.

3

Alexei Leonov
Meeting the Void

*T*he Soviet Vostoks had proved cosmonauts could survive in space. Project Mercury, carried out simultaneously (1961-1963), demonstrated the same thing to the Americans. Now it was time for both superpowers to shoot for the ultimate target—the Moon. There was much work to be done, however. Advanced spacecraft able to rendezvous and dock, and to land on the lunar surface, had to be developed. Crews of two or more had to be trained to fly the new ships; to handle the weightlessness of space long enough to complete a thorough Moon mission (up to two weeks); and to function outside their spacecraft, either "walking" in space or actually walking on the Moon's surface.

Naturally, a race had developed between the superpowers. As of March 19, 1965, the Soviets appeared to be winning. They already had beaten America by orbiting the first artificial satellite (*Sputnik*) in 1957, the first man (Yuri Gagarin) in 1961, and the first woman (Valentina Tereshkova) in 1963. And they had launched the first multi-man crew (of three, aboard *Voskhod 1*) on October 12, 1964. Then came *Voskhod 2*, rocketed into orbit on March 18 and recovered the following day. On that flight, a man (Alexei Leonov) walked in space for the first time. Of course, Soviet accounts of the flight were somewhat less than accurate. For instance, they never mentioned that Leonov almost became the first man to die in space.

Alexei Arkhipovich Leonov was born in Listvyanka, in the Siberian region of the Soviet Union, on May 30, 1934. His father, Arkhip, worked in the copper mines of the nearby Altai Mountains. It was hard work, but no tougher than mother Evdokiya's job—taking care of Alexei and his eight siblings! From an early age, outgoing Alexei displayed unusual artistic talent. Although Arkhip's job paid barely enough to keep the family fed and clothed, he managed to buy his youngest son the paints and brushes he needed. Years later, Alexei would paint pictures of his space flights.

The first multi-person crew, shortly after they returned to Earth in October 1964. They are, from left to right: Konstantin Feoktistov, Vladimir Komarov, and Boris Yegorov. The crew did not wear space suits because there wasn't enough room in the capsule.

Following the end of World War II in autumn 1945, the Leonovs moved westward to Kaliningrad, on the Baltic Sea south of the Soviet republic of Lithuania. There, Alexei graduated from High School Number 21 in spring 1953. As happened to all Soviet men, Alexei was drafted into the military—in this instance, the Soviet Air Force, where he applied for pilot training. It was a spontaneous decision, for Alexei had never expressed any desire to fly. But he loved risks. And once committed to a course of action, he was the type to push ahead with maximum effort. These traits would take him far—indeed, all the way to space. They would also bring him back.

Four years of study at the Chuguyev Military Aviation School in the Soviet republic of Ukraine ended with Alexei Leonov's graduation in 1957. Next for the new pilot was duty with a Russian air force unit in the nation of East Germany (now part of the reunified Federal Republic of Germany). For two and a half years, Leonov flew jets and studied aeronautical engineering at the Zhukovsky Air Force Engineering Academy. He was there in October 1959 when word spread that officials in Moscow were looking for military pilots to fly into space. Leonov made another snap decision. He applied to become a cosmonaut.

Five months later, officials picked Leonov and 19 others to train for the first space missions. At the time Yuri Gagarin flew in April 1961, Leonov was training for the eleventh flight. Soon after Valentina Tereshkova's mission in June 1963, however, all remaining flights of the single-seat Vostok spacecraft were canceled. The order came straight from Moscow, where leader Nikita Khrushchev was demanding something more spectacular than simply orbiting the planet.

From the launch of *Sputnik 1* in October 1957, Khrushchev had pushed ceaselessly to one-up the Americans in space. President John Kennedy of the United

States, who hated to lose just as much as Khrushchev, pushed back. In May 1961, Kennedy committed America to a Moon landing by 1970. As one historian has noted, the superpowers were fighting the Cold War with missiles armed with capsules instead of warheads.

The human Vostok flights brought early victory to the Soviets. The Americans battled back with a series of one-man flights known as Project Mercury. Now they planned several two-man missions to develop the skills and equipment necessary to reach the Moon. These would be part of Project Gemini. Gemini scared Khrushchev. No simple Vostok could match the Gemini spacecraft's ability to rendezvous and dock. The Soviets were building their own advanced spaceship, the three-man Soyuz, but development lagged. Knowing that Gemini would beat Soyuz to space, and that anything Gemini did would outshine Vostok, Khrushchev scrapped Vostok altogether. What he wanted was something more like Gemini. What he got was Voskhod.

Voskhod was little more than "smoke and mirrors." Space chief Sergei Korolev took a single-seat Vostok and stuffed in two extra seats. In this way, he achieved the first group space flight (the three-cosmonaut *Voskhod 1* in October 1964) five months before astronauts Gus Grissom and John Young flew in *Gemini 3*. He expected *Voskhod 2* to steal even more of Gemini's thunder. Korolev knew that NASA had scheduled a space walk for one of its early Gemini crews—perhaps as early as

The small round balls surrounding the one-person Vostok capsule were nitrogen and oxygen tanks supplying life support. The cosmonaut could peer out one small porthole in front of his seat.

summer 1965—so he pushed to have *Voskhod 2* ready for a space-walk mission by March 1965. As things turned out, Korolev pushed too hard. His space walker, 30-year-old Alexei Leonov, would be ready. Leonov's experimental space suit would not be.

Leonov's odyssey began in early 1964, after Khrushchev's cancellation of Vostok. Leonov and Pavel

Belyayev were picked to fly the *Voskhod 2*, which would include the first-ever space walk. Korolev chose Leonov because of the "daring" cosmonaut's "quick-wittedness, liveliness, [and] cleverness." No doubt the space chief recalled the incident a year earlier when a car carrying Leonov and his wife suddenly veered off the road into deep water. Calmly, the cosmonaut freed himself, then saved his wife, Svetlana, and the car's driver.

Leonov found training for *Voskhod 2* especially intense. He and Belyayev (who would be the mission's commander) learned about the spacecraft through hundreds of simulations in capsule mockups. Attached to the side of one of the dummy Voskhods was a collapsible rubber tube, three feet wide and about six and a half feet long. This was a model of the airlock Leonov would float through to reach open space. The Soviets mounted a second mockup inside a transport plane. When the plane flew in huge arches, the two cosmonauts experienced between 30 and 45 seconds of weightlessness. Still another simulator sat inside a decompression (or vacuum) chamber. Wearing a pressurized space suit, Leonov spent hours practicing entering and exiting the capsule's airlock.

The suit itself was a major innovation. Essentially a self-contained mini-spacecraft, it would provide Leonov with everything he needed to survive beyond the hull of *Voskhod 2*. In fact, the garment was an early model of a Soviet Moon suit. Unfortunately, its production was

The two Voskhod 2 *cosmonauts training for their flight; Leonov on the swing and Pavel Ivanovich Belyayev (1925-1970) in the wheel. Belyayev was the oldest and most experienced pilot among the first group of cosmonauts, but injuries and health problems had kept him grounded.*

rushed. Several failures along the way forced design changes. That in itself was not unusual. Experimental designs typically suffer "growing pains" on their way to becoming finished products. In this case, however, the final suit never passed a tryout in space. That was unusual. Robotic test flights, then animal flights (chimpanzees for the United States, dogs for the Soviets), typically preceded actual manned missions. The Soviets tried. They sent a suit up inside a robot spacecraft, but lost all data when the capsule exploded. Any retest, not to mention the follow-up dog flight, would have delayed *Voskhod 2* well into autumn. With astronaut Ed White scheduled to walk in space in June, postponement meant defeat. *Voskhod 2* would launch on schedule.

Leonov and Belyayev lifted off on March 18, 1965. Fifteen minutes later they entered an orbit that eventually pushed them to a record altitude of 302 miles above Earth. Once in orbit, Leonov began breathing pure oxygen. Soviet spacecraft were pressurized with normal air, which contains almost 80 percent nitrogen. Leonov had nitrogen in his blood as a result. If he were suddenly to experience decompression—that is, a sudden drop in the atmospheric pressure surrounding his body—the nitrogen would evaporate, causing bubbles in his blood and body tissue.

"The bends," as decompression sickness is called, could cause painful convulsions and even unconsciousness. To avoid the bends as he floated in the decompressed vacuum of space, Leonov purged the nitrogen from his blood by breathing pure oxygen. After an hour, Leonov made final adjustments to his suit, motioned to Belyayev that he was ready, then swam headfirst into the airlock that extended outward from the capsule's hatch.

Alexei Leonov re-created his crawl through the airlock for a documentary film made after his flight.

The rubberized tube was a tight fit for the cosmonaut and his bulky space suit. As Leonov squeezed inside, Belyayev secured the hatch behind him. The airlock was then depressurized to match the vacuum of space. "This is Diamond," Leonov radioed to Belyayev—he had chosen the hardest of all natural substances as his call sign. "Everything is in order. I feel fine." He then opened the outer hatch.

Although Leonov wore a special visor, he found himself squinting as "a blinding ray of sunlight" flooded the airlock. Cautiously, he grasped the end of the tube and pulled. Then . . . "I stretched out my arms and legs and soared." Passing beneath him like "an enormous colored map" was Earth, brilliantly awash in blues, greens, browns, and whites. The magnificence of the sight nearly overwhelmed him.

Leonov became the first human to step into the vastness of space.

Alexei could clearly make out the fields, mountains, and rivers of the Soviet Union. At the end of his 16-foot tether was *Voskhod 2*, a silvery silhouette against the starry blackness of space. A camera clamped onto the edge of the airlock beamed grainy, black-and-white images of Leonov, seeming to wave, back to Russia. Finally, after 12 short minutes, Belyayev ordered Leonov to return.

According to Leonov's post-flight account, rejoining his commander presented no "particular difficulties." This is not true. (It is likely Soviet authorities demanded Leonov not write the truth.) More likely, the following is what really happened. As Leonov floated back to *Voskhod 2*, he was unaware that his suit's pressure had caused it to balloon more than expected. (There was no way he could have predicted this, since the suit had never been tested in space!) As he had done countless times in training, Leonov grabbed the lip of the airlock and swung his feet up to the opening. He had to enter feet first; otherwise, he'd never be able to reach back and close the hatch. This time, however, as he tried to swing his legs into the opening, Leonov found he could not bend at the waist. In a single sickening instant, he realized he was trapped outside the spacecraft.

Leonov's only hope was to release oxygen—and thus pressure—from the suit. He had to be careful, though; too much reduction would trigger decompression sickness and certain death. Over several minutes, Alexei slowly bled oxygen from the suit. Finally he was able to catch one foot, then two, on the edge of the opening. He wedged his body through, swung the hatch closed, and repressurized the airlock. Once back in the capsule, Leonov strapped himself into his seat, exhausted and covered with sweat. He had lost 12 pounds in just 22 minutes, but he was alive.

He was alive for the time being, anyway. Near the end of the flight the next day, Belyayev discovered that the capsule's automatic guidance and propulsion systems were dead. (The guidance system pointed the craft in the right direction so that when the propulsion system—or retro-rocket—fired, it would slow the craft down and drop it out of orbit.) The good news was, *Voskhod 2* was equipped with backup manual systems. The bad news was, ground controllers ordered Belyayev to fire the manual retro-rocket two seconds too late. The cosmonauts survived the fall to Earth, but their capsule came down about 1,200 miles off course.

More specifically, Leonov and Belyayev came down in a deserted, snow-covered forest in the Ural Mountains. The cosmonauts were cold, so they crawled outside, built a fire, and waited for help to arrive. Night fell after several hours and still there was no sign of a rescue crew. Leonov did catch sight of something else circling through the trees, however—wolves! The two men scurried back into the icy capsule, where they remained until help finally showed up the next morning with food, warm clothes, and skis. They had to ski to the rescue helicopters that had landed in a clearing.

Following the *Voskhod 2* mission, Leonov was promoted to deputy commander of the cosmonauts. In that position, he supervised training in space walks. The primary purpose of space walks, of course, was to develop the equipment and techniques to explore the Moon's surface. In November 1966, Leonov learned he would get that chance. If all went as planned, Alexei Leonov would take humanity's first step on the Moon in late 1967 or early 1968. That never happened, of course. Repeated failures during tests of the spacecraft and its booster rocket kept pushing the lunar missions back. America finally won the race to the Moon when *Apollo 8* slipped into lunar orbit just before Christmas 1968. That was followed by Neil Armstrong's "small step" during the *Apollo 11* mission the following July.

The U.S. victory was especially bitter for Leonov; the Soviets, unwilling to settle for second place, canceled their Moon program altogether. Leonov was transferred to the new Salyut space station project. He and two other cosmonauts were scheduled to make the second flight to the station in June 1971. A week prior to launch, however, crewmate Valeri Kubasov became ill and the reserve crew flew the mission instead. A missed opportunity for Leonov soon turned into another escape from death. Following a three-week stay aboard *Salyut* (the first mission of its kind), the reserve crew suffocated during reentry when a faulty valve bled away the spacecraft's air supply. Again, the Soviets had risked sending cosmonauts into space without space suits. Had it not been for Kubasov's last-minute disqualification, he, Leonov, and Petr Kolodin might have been the three dead cosmonauts.

Leonov and Kubasov next found themselves assigned to command a mission to a second Salyut in August 1972. That mission was scrapped when the unmanned space station blew up during launch in June.

There were seven Salyut space stations, and their success proved that people could live in space.

Amazingly, a third Salyut mission fell through for Leonov and Kubasov in May 1973 after the unoccupied station developed fatal control problems during its first orbit.

Just as Leonov was probably starting to doubt whether he would ever return to space, another opportunity materialized. When U.S. president Richard Nixon had journeyed to Moscow in May 1972 as part of his efforts to reduce tensions with the Soviet Union (a policy known as "détente"), he agreed to a first-ever superpower space mission. The Americans picked Deke Slayton, Tom Stafford, and Vance Brand to fly the mission. The Soviets chose Leonov and Kubasov.

The Apollo-Soyuz Test Project (so named for the American and Soviet spacecraft) started with the successful launchings of the two crews on July 15, 1975. Two days later and 140 miles above western Europe, the Americans and Soviets docked. Three hours later, Stafford and Leonov, floating in the docking tunnel connecting their spacecraft, performed the first superpower handshake in space. Then Leonov passed around tubes of vodka and ordered everyone to drink. With President Gerald Ford watching on television, the startled Americans hesitated. Then they drank, only to realize the smiling Leonov had given them soup. It was a good mission.

The six-day space flight was Alexei's last. Shortly thereafter, he took over as deputy chief of the Gagarin Cosmonaut Training Center. There he trained cosmonauts for missions aboard space stations, including *Mir*,

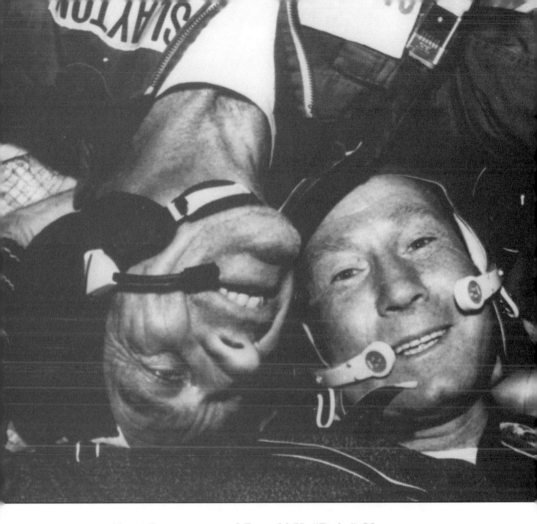

*Alexei Leonov greeted Donald K. "Deke" Slayton
(1924-1993), docking module pilot of the American
crew during the Apollo-Soyuz Test Project.*

launched in February 1986. With the breakup of the
Soviet Union in December 1991, Leonov retired from the
space program and entered private business. He contin-
ues to live in Russia, where he is active in the International
Association of Space Flight Veterans and the International
Astronautic Academy.

A precise pilot who also relied on his instincts, Walter "Wally" Marty Schirra Jr. (b. 1923) was the perfect choice to accomplish the first rendezvous of two orbiting spacecraft.

4

Wally Schirra
Rendezvous with Destiny

*D*uring his years as a test pilot, Wally Schirra didn't just climb into an aircraft—he slipped it on like an old leather jacket. The fit was that comfortable. It had to be. Schirra had to know every detail of the jets he tested— how they reacted in steep climbs or tight turns, or how they handled a sudden loss of power. At speeds faster than 1,500 mph, a single moment when a pilot lost the feel for his aircraft could mean disaster. On December 12, 1965, the veteran jet pilot faced an even greater challenge: to rendezvous his orbiting spacecraft with another.

Schirra never left Earth that day. The countdown proceeded normally as he and copilot Tom Stafford readied themselves for blastoff. The big Titan booster rocket that would push their Gemini capsule into orbit ignited four seconds before launch. But just as it neared maximum power, it died unexpectedly. That was bad. No one liked sitting on a rocket with more than a quarter-million pounds of rocket fuel that wasn't acting the way it was supposed to. Even scarier, a sensor in front of Schirra

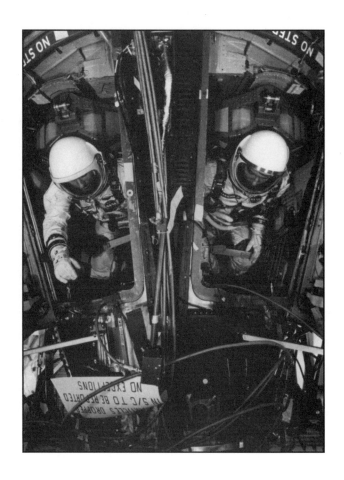

Wally Schirra (right) and Thomas P. Stafford checked out their Gemini 6 *spacecraft two months before the scheduled launch.*

indicated the rocket actually had lifted off a few inches before shutting down. A reading like that meant one of two things. The first was that Schirra and Stafford were about to die. If the Titan had lifted off, it would explode as it settled back to Earth. Schirra should have pulled the ejection handle and sent himself and Stafford free of the impending fireball. But he never did. And neither did Stafford. The rookie astronaut bet his life that Schirra had a pretty good reason for just sitting there.

Schirra had a good reason. It was the other possible explanation for the flashing sensor—that the sensor was wrong. "I had the experience of a Mercury flight," the veteran astronaut later explained, "and my butt told me we hadn't left the pad." It just never occurred to him to eject. Turns out Schirra's gut feeling saved the mission. Had he triggered an ejection, the rocket-powered seats would have charred the inside of the spacecraft and delayed a rendezvous for months. It was almost as if Schirra's participation in the first orbital rendezvous mission was predestined.

Walter "Wally" Marty Schirra Jr. was born in Hackensack, New Jersey, on March 12, 1923. Schirra's father, the first Walter Marty Schirra, had been a combat pilot in World War I. For a time after the war, he and Wally's mother, Florence Shillito Leach, earned their living as "barnstormers," performing stunts in aviation shows. Walter would fly the plane while Florence walked along the wings.

Growing up in Oradell, New Jersey (a small town about 10 miles north of Hackensack), Wally often rode his bike to a nearby airport to watch the airplanes. He especially idolized the pilots in their scarves, goggles, and leather jackets. "I wanted to grow into that image," he recalled.

Schirra graduated from Dwight W. Morrow High School (named after the father-in-law of famous flyer Charles Lindbergh) in June 1940, then entered Newark College of Engineering in Newark, New Jersey. After Japan bombed Pearl Harbor on December 7, 1941, forcing the United States into World War II, Schirra opted to serve his country by fulfilling a childhood dream. He decided to fly planes for the United States Navy and entered the U.S. Naval Academy at Annapolis, Maryland, in autumn 1942.

Schirra graduated in spring 1945, too late to train to fly in World War II. (The war officially ended in September.) He soon got another chance. On June 25, 1950, North Korea invaded South Korea, starting the Korean War. Wally Schirra volunteered for an exchange program with the U.S. Air Force and was flying combat missions over North Korea by early 1951. Over the next eight months, he flew 90 missions and shot down two enemy fighters.

Schirra left Korea in December 1951. The fact that in combat a single lapse of concentration could mean death had given him a new seriousness about flying. He had become determined to be the best, "to go higher, farther, and faster—in the newest jets." The navy assigned him to China Lake in California, a test facility where he flew advanced fighters equipped with an experimental air-to-air missile called the Sidewinder. Schirra was the first navy pilot to test the heat-seeking missile, which is still in service.

Next up for Wally Schirra was duty with a training squadron in San Francisco, California. During 1954-1955, he taught rookie flyers the secrets of surviving combat. In 1955, he deployed to the Far East for a two-year tour of duty aboard the aircraft carrier *Lexington*. Near the end of his assignment, Schirra received great news: he'd been accepted into the navy's test pilot school at Patuxent River, Maryland. He reported to the Naval Air Test Center for training in January 1958.

After graduating, Schirra flew the hottest jets the navy offered. One of those was the F4 Phantom, a brand-spanking-new fighter capable of reaching Mach 2 (twice the speed of sound, about 1,500 mph). It was Schirra's job to determine whether the Phantom was up to navy standards. He loved the assignment. He just wished it would have lasted longer. In February 1959, Schirra received "blind" orders (meaning no reason was given) to report to Washington, D.C. Not until he arrived did he learn their purpose. The National Aeronautics and Space Administration (NASA) was looking for volunteers to fly into space, and someone had thought of Wally Schirra.

NASA was new, created on October 1, 1958, in direct response to the Soviet Union's launching of the first artificial satellite a year earlier. *Sputnik 1* was a great victory for the Soviets. Developing nations, American leaders feared, would now turn to the Soviet Union for technological, scientific, and political guidance instead of to the United States. That would cause a gradual shift in the "balance of power" toward the Communists. *Sputnik's* threat was more immediate, too. A rocket that could launch a satellite into orbit around the world also had the capability to drop a nuclear bomb anywhere along the way. To reaffirm American leadership in technology and weapons, President Dwight Eisenhower and Congress created NASA and ordered it to put a man into space and, most importantly, to do it first.

Of 324 possible candidates from the navy, air force, and marine corps, space officials chose Wally Schirra in April 1959 to become one of America's first seven astronauts. (The other six were John Glenn, Alan Shepard, Scott Carpenter, Leroy "Gordo" Cooper, Virgil "Gus" Grissom, and Donald "Deke" Slayton.) The selection process had been grueling and often humiliating. No one had flown in space, so doctors were unsure how healthy astronauts had to be. They analyzed the pilots' blood, tested samples of their bodily wastes, and photographed every inch of their bodies—even from the inside with X-rays! The pilots ran on treadmills until their sides ached, sweated inside saunas for hours, and

While president of the United States during the 1950s, former World War II general Dwight David Eisenhower (1890-1969) fought a different type of battle, this time against Communism. Establishing NASA was one of his many efforts to stay ahead of Soviet technology and influence.

endured a battery of psychological tests. In the end, few doubted they were the best of the best.

Schirra and the others now began the real training. Like their Soviet counterparts, the Americans endured endless runs on the centrifuge to condition themselves to the increased gravity (g-forces, or g's) they would experience during liftoff and reentry into the atmosphere. And the astronauts had their own version of the Russian "iron maiden," called MASTIF (for Multiple Axis Space Test Inertia Facility). MASTIF was a spherical metal cage, inside which was a seat with a control stick. As the astronauts tumbled, spun, and flipped, they had to use the stick to gain control. As Schirra recalled, "We all lost our cookies or nearly did."

More pleasurable (but sometimes just as nauseating) was the weightlessness training. Transport planes flew huge arches, at the top of which the astronauts floated freely for a half-minute or more. Then there were the precious moments when Schirra and the others could actually sit down, taking classes on physics, space navigation, communications, and astronomy, or during simulations inside the many different spacecraft mockups.

Schirra's least favorite part of the training—other than MASTIF, which everyone despised—was the survival exercises. Worried the astronauts might land hundreds or even thousands of miles off course, NASA trainers forced them to fend for themselves in the humid jungles of Panama, on rafts in the sweltering Gulf of Mexico, or in the scorching dryness of the Nevada desert. Schirra and the others caught and cooked iguanas, distilled drinking water from salty seawater, and sheltered under crude tents fashioned from parachutes.

Al Shepard became the first of the group to fly when a Redstone rocket boosted his Mercury capsule 115 miles into space on May 5, 1961. While he was America's first space traveler, he wasn't *the* first. Yuri Gagarin of the Soviet Union had claimed the honor three weeks earlier with a single orbit around Earth. The Soviets had won

Alan B. Shepard Jr. (1923-1998) spent only 15 minutes in space aboard Freedom 7, *but his flight confirmed that the Mercury capsule design was sound.*

again. In fact, the Americans still didn't catch up to the Soviets with Shepard's flight. His was a suborbital "hop," meaning he was never meant to fly fast enough to achieve orbit. As it turned out, America did not match Gagarin's achievement until astronaut John Glenn flew a three-orbit mission in February 1962.

Scott Carpenter flew the second orbital mission three months later. Then it was Wally Schirra's turn. Carpenter had had trouble conserving fuel during his three orbits. Schirra vowed a perfect flight for his six-orbit mission that lifted off on October 3. Once circling 175 miles above Earth, Schirra put his capsule through a

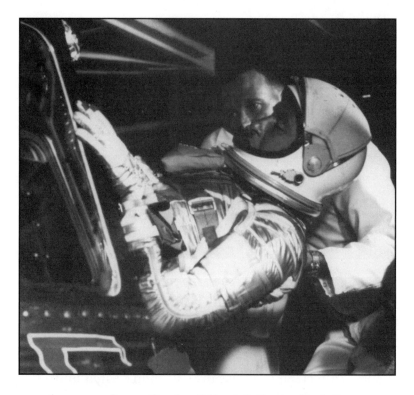

Astronaut Leroy Gordon "Gordo" Cooper Jr. helps Wally Schirra into his Mercury capsule, Sigma 7. *Cooper was Schirra's back-up pilot. If Schirra had been unable to fly, Cooper would have taken his place. All missions have back-up crews who are trained and ready if needed.*

variety of assigned movements. The capsule was not advanced enough to shift from one orbit to another— that is, to move up or down or from side to side—but Schirra was able to roll the craft and to point its nose in various directions. (Nose up or down is known as "pitch," while nose left or right is "yaw.") In fact, so precise was his piloting that he used less than a quarter of his fuel during the mission. Schirra was convinced that given more advanced spacecraft, skilled pilots could rendezvous (fly two ships close together in the same orbit) and then dock (connect to each other).

The ability for two spacecraft to rendezvous and dock was pivotal to the space program. By the time of Schirra's flight, American officials had decided how they would get to the Moon. Astronauts would use a technique called Lunar Orbit Rendezvous (LOR). In LOR, a three-part spacecraft would take off from Earth and fly to the Moon. The spacecraft would have a command capsule housing the astronauts, a service module containing the spacecraft's propulsion system, and a lunar lander. Once in orbit around the Moon, part of the crew would fly the lander down to the surface. They would explore, then fly the lander back to the orbiting command capsule/service module. The parts would rendezvous and dock, the lander would be jettisoned, then the remaining two parts would head for home. Just before getting to Earth, the astronauts would jettison the service module and reenter the atmosphere in the command capsule.

Of course, the simple Mercury capsules would never get astronauts to the Moon. For one thing, they couldn't perform the complex maneuvers in space—like shifting orbits—required to rendezvous and dock. Designers were already working on the Apollo spacecraft astronauts would fly to the Moon. But these ships were several years from being ready, and, in any event, astronauts lacked the skills and techniques to join two spacecraft in orbit. What they needed was an interim project to help them develop the ability. This was one of the reasons behind the Gemini missions of 1965-1966.

"No doubt about it," Schirra recalls, the two-seat Gemini capsule was "the orbital equivalent of a fighter aircraft." Gemini was Schirra's favorite craft, and for good reason: he would use it to make history. It all began on October 25, 1965, the day he and Tom Stafford were set to lift off in *Gemini 6* to perform the first-ever rendezvous and docking. The big day came—and went. The Agena rocket that was to serve as the docking target blew up just minutes after launch. Schirra and Stafford's second shot came on December 12, but their Titan booster fizzled out after barely a second. The crew's decision not to eject saved the mission for another day. They finally launched on December 15.

Schirra's new target was *Gemini 7*, piloted by Frank Borman and Jim Lovell, which had been successfully launched on December 4. As *Gemini 6* entered orbit and began the pursuit, it was more than 1,200 miles behind

Gemini 7. Because Schirra and Stafford were in a lower orbit (168 miles high versus 186 miles), however, they steadily closed the gap. (An object in a higher orbit takes longer to circle a planet than does an object in a lower orbit because the higher object is farther away and travels in a bigger circle.) Besides regular adjustments to altitude, Schirra constantly fired his thrusters to ensure his craft came up directly behind *Gemini* 7 and not off to one side.

Just past five hours into the mission, Schirra spotted a "real bright star" about 60 miles away. It was *Gemini* 7. Two more thruster burns put *Gemini* 6 just 1,000 yards behind the target. With a feather-light touch on the control stick, Schirra slowed his craft, which had been closing on *Gemini* 7. The teamwork between Schirra and Stafford, who was monitoring the computer and calling out distances and speeds, reached its most critical point; even the slightest error could send the two craft slamming together.

After nearly six hours—and some 35,000 thruster burns—Schirra slowed *Gemini* 6 to perfectly match the speed of *Gemini* 7. Often only mere inches separated the two crews as they circled Earth three times. For all intents and purposes, *Gemini* 6 and 7 were now a single ship coasting through space at over 17,500 mph. The first-ever orbital rendezvous was history.

"The whole thing of rendezvous is exquisite timing, delicate little touches," Schirra would later recall. "You had to really get in there and use both hands and pitch and roll and move."

This photograph of Gemini 7 *was taken through the hatch window of* Gemini 6 *during the rendezvous on December 15, 1965. The two capsules traveled at over 17,500 miles per hour about 160 miles above Earth.*

Astronauts now knew it was possible to join two spacecraft in orbit. Other Gemini missions—like Ed White's space walk from *Gemini 4* in June 1965—helped them to perfect additional skills, techniques, and equipment needed to reach the Moon. It was time for Project Apollo. Tragically, before *Apollo 1* flew it was destroyed in a fire during a routine ground test on January 27, 1967.

Astronauts Gus Grissom, Roger Chaffee, and Ed White (the space walker) were killed. Apollo ground to a halt while engineers redesigned the capsule. Meanwhile, officials picked a commander for the orbital test flight of the new spacecraft scheduled for sometime in 1968. Only then could the lunar missions begin. It was just the job for a hot test pilot like Wally Schirra.

During the third orbit of Gemini 4, *Edward H. White II spent 21 minutes outside the craft. The cord swirling in front of him contained both his oxygen line and a tether tying him to the capsule.*

Apollo 7 lifted off from Cape Canaveral, Florida, on October 11, 1968. (*Apollo 4, 5,* and *6* were unpiloted test flights flown in 1967 and 1968. There were no missions *2* and *3*.) Rookie astronauts Walt Cunningham and Donn Eisele joined Schirra in the capsule. For the next 11 days, the crew tested all systems of the new craft. *Apollo* 7 had only a command capsule and service module. The lander would be tested by the crew of *Apollo 9* five months later. Guidance, navigation, and propulsion systems all passed their trials with flying colors. The crew even had time to participate in the first-ever live television broadcast from space. The near-perfect mission ended with *Apollo* 7's splashdown on October 22. Next up in December: *Apollo 8* and the first manned mission to orbit the Moon.

Apollo 7 was Wally Schirra's last flight into space. He retired from NASA on July 1, 1969, and entered private business. For the last 30 years, he has served in a variety of leadership positions for several different corporations and has sat on the boards of directors for many others. Schirra currently works as a private consultant near his home in Rancho Santa Fe, California. He and his wife, Josephine "Jo" Fraser (whom he proposed to after dating for just seven days), have two children: Walter Marty III, born on June 23, 1950; and Suzanne Karen, born on September 29, 1957.

Two weeks after Schirra left the astronaut corps in 1969, Neil Armstrong, Edwin "Buzz" Aldrin, and Mike Collins blasted off in *Apollo 11*, bound for the surface of

The Apollo 7 *crew (left to right): Donn F. Eisele (1930-1987), command module pilot; Wally Schirra, commander; and Walter Cunningham (b.1932), lunar module pilot*

the Moon. Schirra had helped pave the way for the Moon mission. On flights aboard Mercury, Gemini, and Apollo (he was the only astronaut to fly all three), he helped prove the feasibility of Lunar Orbit Rendezvous and the usability of the Apollo spacecraft. He attributes his success to the "harmony" that as a pilot he achieved with the machines he flew. "If you ever achieve exquisite harmony," Schirra has written, "you have reached a level of absolute confidence. Man and machine have become one. There is no limit to what they can do together."

Neil Alden Armstrong (b. 1930) will always be remembered as the first man to walk on the Moon.

5

Neil Armstrong
Magnificent Desolation

*L*ike most test pilots, Neil Armstrong was no stranger to exotic flying machines. Before he joined NASA in 1962, he flew everything from the Paresev (a steerable parachute-type plane) to the X-15 rocket plane (at 4,000 miles per hour!) to simulators of the X-20 (a precursor to the space shuttle that was never built). And like most combat pilots, Armstrong had his share of close calls during the Korean War in the early 1950s. But one of the strangest, most dangerous machines he ever flew was a bug-like, helicopter-sort-of-thing called the Flying Bedstead.

Officially, the Flying Bedstead was the Lunar Landing Training Vehicle. Essentially a four-legged metal frame (hence the nickname), the LLTV was powered by a jet engine with a helicopter cockpit attached. The jet made it hover, while several small thrusters allowed it to move about and land. It was meant to simulate a lander setting down on the Moon. In May 1968, the LLTV crashed, nearly killing Armstrong. He was practicing hovers and descents when the vehicle rolled right, then left, then shot straight up to an altitude of 200 feet. Then it came down. Armstrong ejected to safety just a half-second before the contraption hit the ground and exploded. It was later determined he had run too low on fuel.

Now, 14 months later and a quarter-million miles from home, Armstrong was uncomfortably close to reliving that incident. Here he was, looking for a place to land, flying a bug-like, helicopter-sort-of-thing. And he was running out of fuel. But this was no LLTV, and there was no escape if this contraption went down. He and Buzz Aldrin would die on the Moon.

Neil Alden Armstrong was born near Wapakoneta, Ohio, to Stephen and Viola Armstrong on August 5, 1930. Two years later, Stephen took Neil to an airshow in Cleveland, Ohio. The little boy quickly developed a fascination with airplanes. He even dreamed about flying—or, more specifically, about hovering. "I could, by holding my breath, hover over the ground," recalled Armstrong of the nocturnal visions. "I neither flew nor fell . . . I just

A Lunar Landing Training Vehicle similar to the one flown by Armstrong. This vehicle, piloted by astronaut James A. Lovell Jr. training for Apollo 13, *made a softer landing.*

hovered." When Neil was six, his father took him for an airplane ride for the first time. By age nine, he was building model airplanes and reading "everything I could lay hands on concerning aviation."

Of course, Neil couldn't wait to start flying. Working nights in a bakery to earn the money for lessons, he passed his flight test on his sixteenth birthday. Neil hoped to go to college and study aeronautical engineering, but his parents couldn't afford tuition. So Neil applied for a U.S. Navy scholarship and received one. After graduating from Wapakoneta's Blume High School in 1947, he enrolled at Purdue University in Indiana.

In early 1949, the navy called Neil Armstrong to active duty and sent him to flight school in Pensacola, Florida. When war broke out between North and South Korea in June 1950, Armstrong found himself on a ship to Asia. He flew 78 combat missions off the aircraft carrier *Essex* over the next two years. Not surprisingly, some nearly cost him his life. Once, the wing of his jet clipped a cable the North Koreans had stretched across a valley to damage enemy planes. Armstrong barely coaxed the crippled jet back to the *Essex*. He didn't even make it that far a few months later when his fighter was struck by ground fire. Armstrong just managed to cross into friendly territory before ejecting.

His return home came in spring 1952. He quit the navy, returned to Purdue, and graduated in January 1955 with a degree in aeronautical engineering. Along the way, Armstrong met Janet Shearon. They married in January 1956.

By the time he left Purdue, Armstrong had settled on a career: he would fly the most advanced aircraft he could find. He joined the National Advisory Committee for Aeronautics (NACA) as a research pilot and over the next seven years spent over 4,000 hours in more than 200 different types of jets, helicopters, gliders, and rocket-powered aircraft. The hottest airplane he flew was the hypersonic X-15. Designed to test the effects of "near space" on pilots and aircraft, the X-15 would fly as high as 67 miles (over 354,000 feet) and as fast as Mach 6.72 (4,520 mph) before being phased out in 1968. Armstrong made seven flights in the stub-winged rocket-plane between December 1960 and July 1962. On one of those he flew over 3,800 mph and reached an altitude of 207,000 feet—high enough to see the edge of space.

When NASA (the National Aeronautics and Space Administration, which NACA became in October 1958) started training test pilots to fly into space in 1959, Armstrong thought little of joining their ranks: "We thought we were far more involved in space flight research than the Mercury people." John Glenn's orbital flight in February 1962 opened his eyes. Glenn, after all, traveled three times around the world in less than five hours. Armstrong knew no X-15 would ever match that. He applied to join the astronaut corps.

In September 1962, NASA invited Neil Armstrong and eight other test pilots to join the space program. Armstrong and the others were brought aboard to train for Gemini and Apollo, the follow-up projects to Mercury. The missions of Mercury, NASA's first series of human space flights, were flown until May 1963. NASA's goal for the Mercury program was to prove that astronauts could function in space. The purpose of Gemini was more complex. Procedures for space walks, orbital rendezvous and docking, and long-duration missions of up to two weeks would all be developed during its 12 missions. Once astronauts mastered these tasks, they would be ready to explore the Moon in Project Apollo.

On September 20, 1965, Armstrong was named commander of *Gemini 8.* His and copilot David Scott's mission for the March 1966 flight was to rendezvous and dock with a target rocket. By that time, it was expected that astronauts Wally Schirra and Tom Stafford already would have performed the first rendezvous and docking during a mission in October 1965. Because of a technical problem with their target (it blew up), Schirra and Stafford had their flight delayed until December and then were able to complete only the rendezvous. That meant

*Armstrong
training in
the centrifuge*

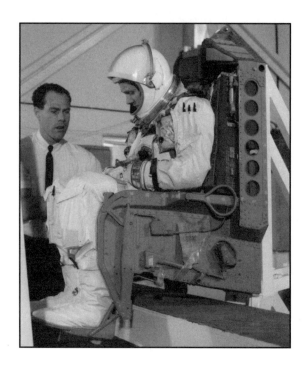

Like Armstrong, astronaut David R. Scott (b. 1932) would later land on the Moon. Scott commanded the Apollo 15 *mission in August 1971.*

Armstrong and Scott had a shot at conducting the first-ever space docking.

Gemini 8's launch went off without a hitch on March 16, 1966. Within six hours, the crew had rendezvoused with the unmanned Agena target rocket. Then came the historic docking—right on the money. For the next 27 minutes, while jubilant flight controllers passed out cigars at Mission Control, Armstrong and Scott quietly went about their business.

Then it started. A slow roll of the combined spacecraft and rocket quickly accelerated into a rapid spiral—like a well-thrown football soaring through orbit. In fact, the Gemini/Agena began spinning sideways like a carousel ride, too. Out of radio contact over the Pacific Ocean, Armstrong manually fired thrusters and regained control.

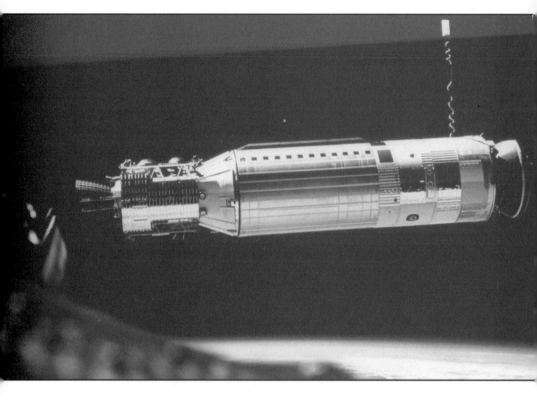

Gemini 8 *was about 45 feet away from the Agena docking target when David Scott took this photograph.*

He thought the problem must be with the Agena rocket, so he undocked.

But the ride grew wilder, which told the astronauts that the problem was their capsule. Armstrong realized that one of the capsule's 16 thrusters must be stuck. Time clearly was running out, so Armstrong shut them all down, and then fired a different set of thrusters used for reentry to regain control. With its spacecraft low on reentry fuel, NASA promptly aborted the rest of the mission and ordered the astronauts home.

It had been a close call. Just a few moments more and the dizzy Armstrong and Scott might have blacked out, followed by the probable breakup of *Gemini 8*. Who knows how long such a disaster would have delayed the space program—and the upcoming Moon missions? But Armstrong and Scott were alive, and both eventually got a chance to put their hard-won skills to the ultimate test.

Just what was so important about rendezvous and docking? The answer is in the method space officials chose to get to the Moon and back: Lunar Orbit Rendezvous. In LOR, astronauts would fly a three-part spacecraft—command capsule, service module, and lunar lander—to the Moon. Once in lunar orbit, part of the crew would ride the lander down to the surface. The lander had separate engines and fuel supplies, one system for descent and the other to leave the Moon. The astronauts would explore the moonscape, then lift off to rendezvous and dock with the "mother ship" orbiting above. Safely back inside the command and service module, the astronauts would jettison the lander and return to Earth.

To test Apollo's systems before attempting the Moon landing, NASA flew 18 unmanned and four manned missions beginning in October 1960. The last rehearsal was *Apollo 10*'s flight in May 1969. On that flight, Eugene Cernan and Thomas Stafford piloted the lunar module— named *Snoopy*—to within nine miles of the surface on

May 21 before rejoining John Young orbiting above in *Charlie Brown*, the command module. They splashed down in the Pacific Ocean five days later. *Apollo 10* had done everything but land. Now it was time for *Apollo 11* to finish the job.

Armstrong had gotten the word in January that he would command the landing, with Buzz Aldrin and Mike Collins rounding out the crew. Six months of intensive training followed. Collins perfected his duties as capsule pilot. Armstrong and Aldrin, who would go down to the surface, practiced landing in several ways. There were ground-based simulators that mirrored the real lander's controls. There was a mock lander suspended above mock craters, where Armstrong and Aldrin practiced descents from 70 feet up. And there was the LLTV, the Flying Bedstead that almost killed Armstrong. When they weren't training to land, Aldrin and Armstrong donned space suits and practiced what they would do after landing—like scooping up Moon rocks and setting up experiments.

Training ended July 15. The next morning, *Apollo 11* lifted off on its way to the Moon. The three-stage Saturn 5 rocket that powered the spacecraft was huge. It stood 364 feet from top to bottom, about the height of a 36-story skyscraper, and weighed almost 6.4 million pounds when fully fueled. The 9 million pounds of thrust generated by its 11 rocket engines (five each in the first two stages and one in the third) was enough to launch the weight of 50 limousines to the Moon.

The Apollo 11 *crew (left to right): Neil A. Armstrong, commander; Michael Collins, command module pilot; and Edwin E. "Buzz" Aldrin Jr., lunar module pilot. The three astronauts began their historic journey the morning of July 16, 1969, lifting off from launch pad 39A at Kennedy Space Center in Florida.*

All three sections of Saturn 5 boosted *Apollo 11* into orbit, with stages one and two dropping off along the way. Once in orbit, the crew checked systems and reignited the third stage. At stage-three burnout, *Apollo 11* was traveling at approximately 24,200 mph— the speed needed to escape Earth's gravitational pull. Now in a "translunar coast" to the Moon, Mike Collins undocked from the third stage and turned the command capsule/service module around in space. He then docked with the lunar lander stowed in the Saturn's third stage. That done, the three-part spacecraft pulled away from the third stage of the Saturn rocket and continued on alone to the Moon.

On July 18, *Apollo 11* entered the gravitational pull of the Moon. The crew were now more than 214,000 miles from home. When they entered lunar orbit on July 19, Aldrin and Armstrong began preparations for undocking the lander.

The lander, *Eagle*, began its descent to the Moon's surface the following day. *Eagle* had no seats. Aldrin and Armstrong stood, secured by harnesses, and for several minutes the astronauts actually flew backward and face down to the Moon's surface. Eight minutes into the descent, the lander pitched to a heads-up, forward-look-ing position so its radar could "read" the surface. At 10 minutes, Armstrong and Aldrin could see their landing site in the Sea of Tranquility, a large plain on the Moon's surface, four and a half miles ahead.

This command/service module, orbiting around the Moon, is passing over the Sea of Tranquility, a relatively level portion of the Moon's surface that ancient astronomers mistook for a body of water. Eagle's landing site was in this plain.

As they came closer, Armstrong realized *Eagle*'s radar was sending them into a "football field-size crater" surrounded by boulders. Even so, he was tempted to land; the craft's descent engine was down to 60 seconds of fuel. Armstrong fought the urge and slowed the lander to a hover 65 feet above the surface. Just as he had dreamed as a child, he crept along, looking for someplace—anyplace—to land.

Then Armstrong saw his spot, a relatively smooth patch amid boulders and craters. Drifting sideways, then backwards, *Eagle* descended into a cloud of dust kicked up by its engine. Thirty seconds of fuel remained, then 25. Buzz Aldrin's voice came over the line: "Forward. Drifting right . . . contact light. Okay, engine stop." It was Neil Armstrong who spoke next to Mission Control: "Houston, Tranquility Base here. The *Eagle* has landed."

Although it looks awkward and flimsy, the lunar module was specially designed for the low-gravity, no-atmosphere environment on the Moon.

Armstrong and Aldrin had five hours to prepare for their historic moon walk. Among their tasks was donning the helmets, gloves, and backpacks that would be their life support systems on the surface. Finally, it was time to depressurize the cabin and open the hatch. Because of the internal layout of *Eagle*, NASA officials months earlier had decided it would be easier for Armstrong to exit first. He backed out on hands and knees toward the ladder that ran down one of the lander's legs. He paused at the bottom, just inches from the surface. Then he stepped free. "That's one small step for a man, one giant leap for mankind." (At least that's what he meant to say. People on Earth heard "one small step for man," the "a" lost in the excitement of the moment or in the transmission.)

To Buzz Aldrin, who joined Armstrong 15 minutes later, the sight was one of "magnificent desolation." The barren, tannish-gray soil extended in every direction. But now was time to work. Aldrin set up several scientific experiments and took photos of the lander from all angles. Armstrong hopped about scooping up some 50 Earth-pounds of rocks. The two set up an American flag, a symbol of the nation's victory in the race.

After about two hours on the surface, the astronauts reentered the lander. They ate, got some much-deserved sleep, then ignited *Eagle*'s small ascent engine to blast themselves back into orbit. Once Armstrong and Aldrin were back aboard *Columbia*—the command capsule—Collins jettisoned the lander and turned the ship earthward.

Neil Armstrong photographed Buzz Aldrin after Aldrin joined him on the surface of the Moon. The vehicle and Armstrong are both reflected in Aldrin's visor.

The crew returned July 24. Months of ticker-tape parades and public appearances followed. *Apollo 11* was Armstrong's last trip into space. He joined NASA Headquarters in Washington, D.C., where he coordinated and managed NASA's aircraft research as deputy associate administrator for aeronautics. Armstrong left the space program for good in August 1971.

For the next eight years, he served as professor of aerospace engineering at the University of Cincinnati and lived on his farm in nearby Lebanon, Ohio. When Armstrong left the school in 1979, he began a career in business, serving as chairman of the board of three corporations. In 1986, NASA named Armstrong vice-chairman of the committee investigating the January 1986 explosion of the space shuttle *Challenger*. Today, Neil Armstrong is retired and lives on his Ohio farm.

The Apollo 11 *command module was recovered by the U.S.S.* Hornet *after parachuting through Earth's atmosphere and splashing down in the Pacific Ocean on July 24, 1969.*

John Watts Young (b. 1930) flew on both Gemini and Apollo missions before commanding the first flight of the space shuttle Columbia.

6

John Young
The Reusable Astronaut

*L*ooking back, Donald K. "Deke" Slayton called John Young one of the "unsung heroes" of the U.S. space program, "a real hardworking guy" who would stick around "as long as there was flying to do." Compliments like these meant something coming from Deke Slayton. As America's chief astronaut during the 1960s and 1970s, Slayton assigned the others their missions. Rock-steady John Young was one of his favorites—Slayton sent him on four flights, including two to the Moon. Young's workload didn't lighten much when Slayton left Flight Crew

Operations in 1974. Young commanded the maiden flight of *Columbia*, the first reusable spacecraft, in 1981 and a second shuttle mission in 1983. That made six space flights in all, more than anyone else until well into the 1990s. Indeed, Young remained eligible for space missions even as NASA moved into the twenty-first century. Slayton was right. If there was flying to do, John Young would be there to do it.

On September 24, 1930, John Watts Young was born in San Francisco, California. The Great Depression had just begun to grip the nation. Shortly before John's second birthday, his father, Hugh, moved the family to Orlando, Florida, in hopes of making a better life for the Youngs. Little could he imagine that his son would one day make history just 50 miles away at Cape Canaveral.

John's love of flying was sparked by Hugh. When the United States entered World War II in December 1941, Hugh Young joined the navy as a Seabee. (Seabee— or "C.B."—is short for "Construction Battalion." Seabees built facilities like harbors and airfields.) It was Hugh's war stories of American fighter planes and German V-2 ballistic missiles that fired John's imagination. Soon the boy was reading everything he could find about rockets and airplanes.

Actually, John loved to read—period. He graduated from Orlando High School in spring 1948 with A's in every course. Also an athlete, John ran track and played on the football team. Friends considered him a class leader.

In fall 1948, John entered the Georgia Institute of Technology (Georgia Tech) in Atlanta. Because he hoped to fly jets for the navy someday, John studied aeronautical engineering—the science of aircraft design and operation. It was a perfect choice. John graduated from Georgia Tech with highest honors in 1952.

He wasted no time joining the navy. Flight school had to wait, however, until John Young had served at least a year aboard ship. Finally, in mid-1953, he began training to fly. Young graduated two years later, qualified to fly jets, propeller planes, and helicopters.

For the next four years, Young flew some of the newest fighter jets in the navy. It only whet his appetite for more. He gained admission to the U.S. Navy Test Pilot School at Patuxent River, Maryland, in January 1959. Test piloting is all about pushing the most advanced aircraft to their design limits. But test pilots don't just climb into the cockpit and punch the accelerator. Everything from takeoff speed to in-flight maneuvers to the angle of attack at landing is carefully preselected and planned. It was this type of demanding precision flying that Young relished.

Young graduated from the test pilot school in December 1959, and for the next three years, Patuxent River was his home as he tested aircraft for the Naval Air Test Center. One of his jobs was to evaluate the weapons systems on F8 Crusaders and F4 Phantoms. Young also traveled to California to participate in Project High Jump.

Strapped into the ejection seat of an F4, Young had to fly the plane as high as possible in the least amount of time. In one record-setting attempt in 1962, he pushed the jet to 80,000 feet in under four minutes.

High Jump was a great thrill. Indeed, Young loved every minute of his job, no matter where or what he flew. But he couldn't help noticing that the test pilots over at NASA were flying higher and faster than he ever would in an aircraft. When word went out that NASA was looking for more astronauts, Young applied. In September 1962, NASA announced its second set of astronauts. Neil Armstrong, who would become the first person to walk on the Moon, was one of the nine chosen. John Young, who would quietly amass the longest list of space "firsts," was another.

Young and his family (Barbara, whom he had married in 1955; Sandra, born in 1957; and John Jr., born in 1959) moved to Houston, Texas, where the astronauts trained at NASA's Manned Spacecraft Center (renamed the Lyndon B. Johnson Space Center after the former president's death in 1973). Young and the others were brought on board for Projects Gemini and Apollo. Gemini, an advanced two-man version of the simple Mercury capsule, would have the added ability to maneuver in orbit. With more mobility, astronauts would train to rendezvous and dock with other spacecraft, a prerequisite for any trip to the Moon. Gemini missions would also include space walks and extended space flights of up to two weeks. Once astronauts gained proficiency in these areas—rendezvous and docking, space walking, and long-duration flights—they would be ready to go to the Moon in Project Apollo.

Young was the first of the new nine to be assigned a flight. In April 1963, Deke Slayton, the chief astronaut in charge of crew assignments, teamed Young with Mercury veteran Virgil "Gus" Grissom for the first manned Gemini mission. *Gemini 3* blasted off on March 23, 1965,

Virgil "Gus" Grissom (1926-1967), one of the original seven astronauts, was the second American in space. He piloted a suborbital Mercury flight on July 21, 1961, in the capsule Liberty Bell 7.

John Young performed the preflight checks, then the hatch was closed and Gemini 3 lifted off, boosted by a Titan rocket.

for a five-hour flight. As *Life* magazine noted at the time, it was a "lift-off to a new era in space." For starters, it was America's first multi-astronaut mission. *Gemini 3* also maneuvered in orbit for the first time. Aided by an onboard computer—another first—Young called out coordinates for Grissom, who then fired the ship's thrusters to move up, down, and sideways. Precision flying was necessary to dock with other spacecraft. Young pulled another first out of his hat, too—well, actually, out of his pocket. As Grissom prepared a meal of bland space food, Young fished out a smuggled corned-beef sandwich. Grissom laughed, but NASA officials weren't so amused. Young received a formal reprimand on his record.

Fortunately, Deke Slayton laughed at the sandwich gag, too. He sent Young up again in July 1966 as commander of *Gemini 10*. NASA had come a long way since Young's first Gemini flight. Ed White of *Gemini 4* had made America's first space walk in June 1965. By the end of the year, *Gemini 6*'s Wally Schirra and Tom Stafford had successfully rendezvoused with Frank Borman and James Lovell in *Gemini 7*. Neil Armstrong and Dave Scott built on that success by docking *Gemini 8* with an unmanned Agena target rocket in March 1966. Now, in *Gemini 10*, Young and crewmate Michael Collins went even farther—literally. They docked twice with two separate Agenas, then used one of the target's engines to blast the joined craft to a new record altitude of 475 miles.

For an encore, Collins made two space walks. After three days in orbit, the astronauts splashed down on July 21.

Project Gemini ended after the twelfth mission in November 1966. Astronauts were now ready to try for the Moon. Tragedy struck almost immediately when a fire inside the spacecraft killed the *Apollo 1* crew members Gus Grissom, Ed White, and Roger Chaffee during a ground test of their capsule in January 1967. Apollo screeched to a halt while engineers redesigned the space-craft. Manned missions resumed with the near-perfect flight of *Apollo* 7 in October 1968. NASA decided to send the next mission all the way to the Moon. Two

The exterior of Apollo 1 *following the fire that killed the three astronauts who were testing the spacecraft. Between* Apollo 1 *and 7, there were three unpiloted test flights,* Apollo 4, 5, *and 6. NASA skipped numbers 2 and 3.*

The Apollo 10 *crew shortly before their successful mission (left to right): Eugene A. Cernan, lunar module pilot; John W. Young, command module pilot; and Thomas P. Stafford, commander*

months later, *Apollo 8* astronauts Frank Borman, Jim Lovell, and William Anders were eating Christmas dinner in lunar orbit.

In March 1969, while in Earth orbit, the crew of *Apollo 9* completed the first piloted test flight of the lunar module. Then a full dress rehearsal had to be run. That frustrating task fell to Tom Stafford, Gene Cernan, and John Young of *Apollo 10*. Between May 18 and 26, 1969, the crew performed every task necessary for a lunar landing except the landing itself. Stafford and Cernan piloted the lander—*Snoopy*—to within nine miles of the Moon's surface, while Young orbited above in *Charlie Brown*, the command capsule. Once Stafford and Cernan had returned, Young jettisoned the lander and blasted *Charlie Brown* on a return path to Earth.

The success of *Apollo 10* cleared the way for Neil Armstrong's *Apollo 11* crew to land on the Moon in July. Six lunar missions followed. "Hardworking" John Young commanded the fifth—*Apollo 16*, which lifted off on April 16, 1972. Three days and a quarter-million miles later, Young, Thomas Mattingly, and Charles Duke slipped into lunar orbit. For Young, it was another milestone: no one before him had orbited the Moon on two different occasions. (Only one other person would— Gene Cernan, commander of *Apollo 17*.) Twenty-three hours later, Young and Duke boarded *Orion* (the lander) and began their 67-mile descent. Mattingly remained behind in *Casper* (the command capsule).

Over the next three days, Young and Duke spent over 20 hours traversing the moonscape. And they did it in style! *Apollo 15*'s crew had used the lunar rover, an electric buggy, for the first time in July 1971. Young and Duke now drove their own rover among the deep craters and steep slopes of the Descartes Highlands. When the time came to leave, the Moon walkers signed off with a short event Young styled the "lunar Olympics." Millions watched on television as Young and Duke jumped up and down and took turns throwing their equipment as far as they could. The items left behind were no longer needed and might have weighed them down during liftoff. The remote video camera still rolled as *Orion* rocketed free of the surface. Four days later, April 27, *Casper* burned through Earth's atmosphere to a successful splashdown.

Young and Duke used a "rover" (Lunar Roving Vehicle) to visit several craters, including the North Ray Crater, which is three-quarters of a mile wide and 650 feet deep—the largest crater explored by astronauts on the Moon.

John Young had now been an astronaut for a decade. He'd flown four times, two each on Gemini and Apollo. He had been the first astronaut to fly who was not one of the original "Mercury Seven." He had been one-half of America's first multi-man crew, had used the first computer in space, had been the first pilot to rendezvous and dock with two different orbital targets, and had been the first person to orbit the Moon on different missions. Finally, Young was one of only 12 people to have walked on the lunar surface (and one of six to have driven on it!). Only Jim Lovell, commander of *Apollo 13*, had as many space flights to his credit. But Lovell was now retired. With more flying left to do, John Young wasn't quitting yet.

Even as *Apollo 16* coasted moonward in 1972, NASA officials were selecting the design of America's next spacecraft. Sometime before 1980, they hoped, the space shuttle would fly. It would lift off vertically like a Saturn Moon rocket for operations in Earth's orbit, then return to land horizontally like an airplane. Except for its large external fuel tank, which would fall away as the ship reached orbit, the shuttle would be completely reusable. These features promised cheaper launches of satellites and people than single-use "throwaway" rockets like Saturn. In January 1973, NASA charged Young to head the space shuttle branch of the astronaut office. It was his job to provide an astronaut's point of view as to what the shuttle should include. Furthermore, it was his responsibility to train the astronauts who would pilot the big orbiter.

Young learned in March 1978 that he would command the shuttle's first flight, scheduled to launch within 12 months. Repeated setbacks in the development of the ship—dubbed *Columbia*—kept pushing the date back. The biggest problem was the shuttle's three main engines. They kept burning up in tests. These main engines were unlike any others ever built. Because of weight constraints, they had to produce 50 percent more power or "thrust" than a similar-sized Saturn engine. They also had to be reusable and their power output adjustable. Conventional rocket engines, like those on the Saturn, were used only once and only at maximum thrust.

Just as frustrating was development of the heat shield. Mercury, Gemini, and Apollo craft had used a coating of epoxy resin that actually burned off during reentry. As it cooked away, it took the heat of reentry with it. Similar single-use shields wouldn't work for a reusable shuttle. A permanent shield was needed. The new system involved covering the orbiter with approximately 31,000 tiles, of which 24,000 were cut into six-inch squares and 7,000 sized to eight-inch squares. The material itself wasn't new. It was silica, the hard, glassy mineral found in sand. When mixed with clay and water, the substance became remarkably resistant to heat. Now the bad news. It took one worker a month to install just seven tiles. Even worse, the darn things kept falling off. When

A technician replaces one of the missing tiles on
Columbia *after the shuttle's delivery to Kennedy*
Space Center in 1979.

Columbia rode piggyback atop a 747 jetliner to Kennedy
Space Center in March 1979, hundreds of the tiles fell off.
If that had been a reentry and the errant tiles had covered
the wings or tail, the shuttle could have been destroyed.

What made the whole situation even scarier was
that *Columbia* would be the first American spacecraft to
carry pilots on its first flight. Mercury, Gemini, and
Apollo spacecraft had all flown into orbit unoccupied
prior to being "man rated." Not the shuttle. NASA was

gambling that *Columbia*'s countless systems and subsystems would work smoothly the first time out. They did test the craft's ability to fly in Earth's lower atmosphere and then land with a prototype shuttle, the *Enterprise*. It was essentially a huge glider.

With all of the bugs finally worked out (NASA hoped!), the countdown proceeded. On April 12, 1981— 20 years to the day after Yuri Gagarin's historic first flight—*Columbia* was launched. At 122 feet long and

The space shuttle Columbia *on the mobile launch platform that moved the shuttle more than three miles from the vehicle assembly building to the launch pad*

214,000 pounds, it was the largest spacecraft ever, approximately the size of a DC-9 commercial airplane. But the orbiter was just a third of what roared off the launch pad. On its belly rode a fuel tank 153 feet long and filled with over a half million gallons of liquid hydrogen and liquid oxygen. This liquid fuel fired the shuttle's main engines. Affixed to the sides of the fuel tank were two solid-propellant rocket boosters, each 149 feet long and filled with 1.1 million pounds of propellant. These worked in tandem with the shuttle's engines to provide the necessary thrust to lift the ship.

For two minutes, boosters and engines pushed *Columbia* ever faster and higher. Thirty-three miles up, the boosters burned out and parachuted back to Earth to be reused. The shuttle's main engines continued burning another six and a half minutes. When they, too, fell silent, *Columbia* was 91 miles above Earth and traveling east at about 17,000 mph. Young jettisoned the external fuel tank to allow it to burn up in the atmosphere, then fired two smaller orbital maneuvering engines to boost the shuttle to an orbital speed of 17,500 mph.

Young had remained remarkably calm during *Columbia*'s thunderous ascent. "Well, the view hasn't changed any," he quipped to copilot Robert Crippen as they surveyed the world from 170 miles up. It was no act of bravado. While Crippen's pulse rate had shot up to 130, about normal for a space flight rookie, Young's hovered near a relaxed 85.

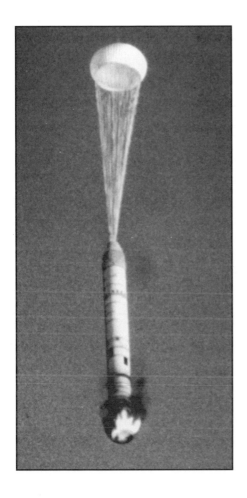

One of the two solid rocket boosters from the space shuttle Columbia *parachutes into the Atlantic Ocean. Ships then retrieve the boosters and tow them back to Cape Canaveral to be reused in another launch.*

Over the next two days, Young and Crippen put the orbiter through its paces. They opened and closed the payload, or cargo, bay doors and tested the maneuvering thrusters. Eight hours into the flight, Young could report the orbiter was performing "like a champ." Of course, the crew also checked systems for sleeping, personal hygiene, and eating. At one point, Crippen even pulled out a corned-beef sandwich!

Finally, two days into the mission, Young instructed the flight computer to turn the ship around so it was traveling tail first. He fired the orbital maneuvering engines, now facing forward, for two and a half minutes. That was enough to slow *Columbia* and drop it out of orbit. With the aid of the computer, Young flipped the spacecraft around and guided it down through the atmosphere. The shuttle now became the world's biggest glider as it soared silently back to earth through the scorching 2,700° F heat of reentry. Following a series of S-turns to reduce airspeed, *Columbia* touched down and rolled to a stop on the main runway at Edwards Air Force Base, California.

The shuttle's success meant there would be many future space flights. Young, now a veteran of a record five space flights, stuck around. On November 28, 1983, he commanded *Columbia* on the ninth shuttle mission, the first to carry six crew members—including the first non-U.S. crew member, German physicist Ulf Merbold. The flight was also the maiden voyage of *Spacelab*, an orbital laboratory carried aloft in the shuttle's payload bay. For 10 days, the astronauts conducted experiments in biology, physics, astronomy, microgravity, and materials processing. So fruitful was their research, in fact, that the crew gathered perhaps 50 times the data produced during all three Skylab missions a decade earlier.

In September 1985, Young was named to a seventh space mission—to deliver the Hubble Space Telescope to orbit in September 1986. The flight never materialized.

Spacelab is deployed from the payload bay during Columbia's ninth mission. The payload bay, located in the center of the orbiter, opens up to space. The bay is 60 feet long, 15 feet wide, and can carry up to 65,000 pounds of cargo.

On January 28, 1986, the shuttle *Challenger* exploded soon after liftoff, killing all seven astronauts aboard. All missions were temporarily scrubbed. NASA reassigned Young in May 1987 as special assistant to the director of Johnson Space Center. It was his job to provide advice on matters regarding the safety, operation, and design of all NASA space initiatives, including the shuttle and the new International Space Station. Since February 1996, Young has served as a JSC associate director. He remains eligible for space flight.

Eileen Marie Collins (b. 1956) worked hard to become an accomplished air force pilot and instructor, but her dream was to travel in space. She not only achieved her goal, but also became the first woman to command a spacecraft.

126

7

Eileen Collins
No News is Good News

Space shuttles are many things. They're reusable. An orbiter can fly at least 100 times during its lifetime. Shuttles are flexible. They transport crews, satellites, telescopes, even space stations to and from orbit. (That's why they're called shuttles.) They sometimes carry portable laboratories in their cargo bays, inside which astronauts perform various experiments. Shuttles even serve as orbital launch pads for deep-space probes.

NASA's orbiters are steadily becoming something else, too—routine. This might be considered a bad thing.

After all, the more routine things become, the less they're noticed. On the other hand, "routine" suggests reliability and effectiveness. Consider commercial air travel. It's routine because it's safe and it works. There are exceptions, of course, sometimes tragic. It's usually then that people take notice. In this sense, the old saying fits: "no news is good news."

A space shuttle shortly after launch. The shuttle has three main parts: the orbiter, the large external tank that holds the fuel, and the two solid rocket boosters. There are four orbiters currently in service, Atlantis, Columbia, Discovery, *and* Endeavor. *The shuttles have flown more than 100 missions since 1981.*

On July 23, 1999, the space shuttle *Columbia* once again grabbed the public's attention, just as it had during its first flight 18 years earlier. No, it didn't crash. But the old routine was disrupted. For the first time aboard any spacecraft, a woman was in charge. And interestingly, this woman, Colonel Eileen Collins of the U.S. Air Force, would rather she had not made the news at all.

Eileen Marie Collins was born in Elmira, New York, on November 19, 1956. Of her parents, James and Rose Marie Collins, Eileen recalled they were always "very supportive" of her and her two brothers and sister. It was James who first sparked Eileen's interest in aviation by taking her to the airport on weekends to watch the planes take off and land. Elmira is the site of Harris Hill, a field well known to the region's glider pilots. Eileen spent summers watching the gliders soar silently overhead. "I always thought that someday I wanted to do that," she remembered.

When she was growing up, Eileen's favorite subjects were math and science. She also read a great deal of history. "I began reading voraciously about famous pilots," she recalled, "from Amelia Earhart to Women's Air Force Service Pilots (WASP) who played an important role in World War II. Their stories inspired me. I admired the courage of these women to go and fly into dangerous situations."

After earning a high school diploma from Elmira Free Academy in spring 1974, Collins studied at nearby

*During World War II, Women's Air Force Service
Pilots tested repaired airplanes and delivered military
aircraft, becoming an essential part of the war effort.*

Corning Community College until 1976, then at Syracuse
University in Syracuse, New York, until 1978. Her two
years at Syracuse went by quickly. Besides studying math
and economics, Collins was a member of the campus
R.O.T.C. (Reserve Officers' Training Corps) and held
several part-time jobs. Her jobs—one of which was waiting tables at a pizza joint—earned her enough money to
pay for flying lessons. She left Syracuse with degrees in
math and economics, and a license to fly gliders.

Collins joined the U.S. Air Force soon after graduation. She was determined to make flying her career, but not just any kind of flying. Collins wanted to fly into space. It had been a dream of hers since childhood, when she first followed the daring astronauts of Project Gemini. "I started learning about the astronauts and their backgrounds," she recalled of that time, "and figuring out what you needed to do to become an astronaut." (That's probably why she worked so hard in math and science!) But while Collins was growing up, it could be only a dream. Astronauts were men. That changed in 1978, when NASA first selected women for space travel. From that moment, Collins knew she had a realistic shot at becoming an astronaut.

Over the next several years, she worked to gain the knowledge and experience she needed to make the astronaut corps. Collins's first step was to train to fly military aircraft. Good grades and flying experience helped her qualify for flight school at Vance Air Force Base in Oklahoma. Collins was among the very first female air force aviators since the WASPs of World War II. Only two years earlier, in 1976, had the air force again opened its flight school to women. After getting her wings in 1979, she stayed at Vance for three years teaching others to fly.

Early in 1983, the air force transferred Collins to Travis Air Force Base in California. She was assigned to fly C-141s, big transports that carried equipment and vehicles, or hundreds of airborne soldiers. During the U.S. invasion of the Caribbean nation of Grenada in October 1983, Collins became one of the first women to fly a combat mission when she delivered a planeload of paratroops. On her return trip, she carried 36 medical students whom the Americans had invaded the Caribbean island to rescue. Following the mission, Collins continued at Travis as an instructor pilot for the C-141.

Collins left Travis in 1985 for a year of graduate study at the Air Force Institute of Technology in Dayton, Ohio. Just as in high school, when she devoured the biographies of famous flyers, Collins again was surrounded by the history of flight. The home of the Air Force Institute of Technology is Wright-Patterson Air Force Base, named for Frank Patterson, a noted test pilot in the 1930s, and Wilbur Wright, who with brother Orville made the first airplane flight in 1903. Her sojourn in Dayton helped Collins earn a master's of science degree in 1986.

From Dayton, Collins transferred to the U.S. Air Force Academy in Colorado to teach cadets as an assistant professor of mathematics. She was never far from her students; when Collins wasn't teaching them math, she was teaching them to fly. Remarkably, she also found time to earn a second master's degree, this one in space systems management. It was at the academy that Collins married Pat Youngs, a fellow officer and pilot she had known since her days at Travis AFB.

In 1989, military officials sent Collins back to California to attend the Air Force Test Pilot School at Edwards Air Force Base. Test pilots are among the elite of all flyers. It's their job to determine whether or not aircraft are ready for military service, a challenge that routinely places their lives at risk. Collins was just the second female pilot to gain admission to the school. Completion of the year-long course would allow her to join a select group of aviators that included Neil Armstrong, Wally Schirra, and John Young—test pilots who became the astronauts she admired as a child. But Collins had long determined to share more than just the sky with her idols. She applied to NASA for shuttle training.

By January 1990, Collins had logged over 5,000 hours in 30 different types of aircraft, totals that would make any astronaut proud. (Schirra logged 3,800 hours, for instance; Neil Armstrong, 4,000; and John Young, an extraordinary 11,500.) Just as important, Collins was a seasoned flight instructor; an experienced commander of large, crew-served aircraft (C-141s); and an accomplished scholar of math and science. She felt she had acquired the hands-on experience and technical know-how to join the space program. NASA agreed. Collins was invited to join the agency as an astronaut candidate.

An intensive, year-long "basic-training" course began in June. Not surprisingly, science dominated the classroom curriculum. Trainees studied math, guidance and navigation, astronomy, physics, and meteorology.

Instructors also lectured on how to perform shuttle maintenance, stow equipment, and discard waste—all tasks in the basic operation of the shuttle.

Beyond the classroom, there were various simulators to pit candidates against any number of computer-generated spacecraft malfunctions. Training in weightlessness took much of their time. Transport planes flew huge arches through the sky, providing trainees with about 30 seconds of microgravity in which to practice eating,

Eileen Collins posed by this T-38 trainer jet, one of the many different aspects of her NASA training.

drinking, and handling space tools. Another way to mimic the weightless environment of space was in the training center's 25-foot-deep "neutral buoyancy" water tank. Here the fledgling astronauts donned space suits and worked on submerged mockups of the shuttle. Collins and the other pilots spent additional time simulating shuttle takeoffs and landings in specially modified aircraft.

In July 1991, Collins graduated from the basic course to become a full-fledged astronaut. Moreover, she had qualified to pilot the shuttle—the first woman to do so. (Previous female astronauts had performed non-flying tasks as either mission specialists or payload specialists.) But Collins's first trip into space had to wait. First came several months of advanced training, covering every aspect of shuttle operations. Once through with that, she worked on various jobs associated with shuttle missions, like fine-tuning takeoff and landing procedures and serving as the spacecraft communicator during several missions. (The spacecraft communicator—called the CAPCOM for "capsule communicator"—is a holdover from the early days of human space flight. During a mission, one of the astronauts not actually flying served as a relay between ground controllers at Mission Control and the capsule crew in space.)

Collins finally got her shot in February 1995. She flew into orbit aboard the shuttle *Discovery* on the first of several joint missions with the Russians and their space station *Mir*. As pilot, Collins guided the orbiter to within 30 feet of *Mir*, carefully utilizing the shuttle's 46 maneuvering thrusters to perform a careful fly-around. It was the first time Americans had seen *Mir*. Collins's task, however, was not to dock with the station, but rather to rehearse the maneuver for the next shuttle mission. Other highlights of the flight included a space walk, deployment and retrieval of a telescope, and several science experiments. After 129 orbits and almost three million miles traveled, *Discovery* returned to Earth on February 11. Collins did not actually land the craft. That duty falls to the shuttle commander.

Twenty-seven months later, Collins returned to space on another flight as pilot of the shuttle *Atlantis*. This trip, STS-84 (Space Transportation System Mission 84), included a stop to resupply *Mir*. Collins again rendezvoused with the station, then docked. Shuttles don't dock nose-first, like the old Gemini or Apollo capsules, but rather payload-bay-first. As they can't see the payload bay, pilots must rely solely on instruments to dock. *Atlantis* dropped off its cargo, four tons in all, then departed to complete its own tasks of science experiments. The nine-day, 3.8-million-mile trip ended on May 24, 1997.

Collins had now flown two times as a pilot, a prerequisite for mission command. In March 1998, NASA named her commander of STS-93, a five-day mission to deploy the Chandra X-ray Observatory. Named for Indian-American Nobel Prize winner Subrahmanyan

The orbiter Atlantis *photographed during the process of undocking from* Mir. *The space station circled Earth from 1986 to 2001, ten years longer than the Russians had anticipated it could stay in orbit.*

Chandrasekhar, the Chandra observatory (or telescope) was designed to help astronomers view such deep-space mysteries as exploding stars, quasars, and black holes. At 45 feet long by 64 feet wide, and almost 13,000 pounds, Chandra would also be the largest and heaviest load ever hauled into space aboard a shuttle. Luckily, former C-141 instructor-pilot Eileen Collins knew a thing or two about delivering cargo.

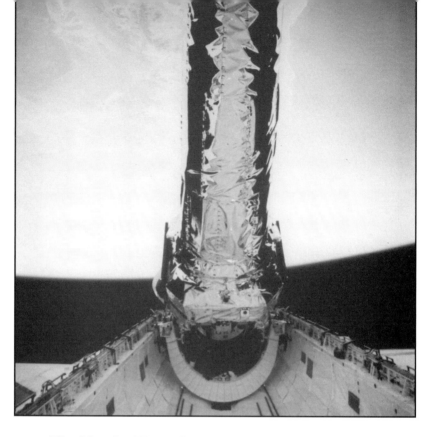

The Chandra X-ray Observatory just before it was released from Columbia's *payload bay. Chandra now orbits high above Earth, over one-third of the way to the Moon. If humans could see as well as Chandra, they could read a stop sign from a distance of 12 miles.*

Columbia roared into orbit on July 23, 1999. Almost immediately, Collins and her four crew members set to work running several hours of predeployment checks on the observatory. Seven hours into the mission and some 175 miles above Southeast Asia, astronaut Catherine "Cady" Coleman activated six springs that pushed the big telescope free of *Columbia*'s payload bay. Collins guided the orbiter on a quick fly-around of the observatory, then hit the maneuvering thrusters again to propel *Columbia* to a safe distance. That was important. About one hour after leaving the shuttle, Chandra's onboard booster rocket ignited to hurl the observatory to its final orbit 85,000 miles above Earth. *Columbia*'s mission had been accomplished.

Four days later, the venerable orbiter burned through the atmosphere on its return voyage to Kennedy Space

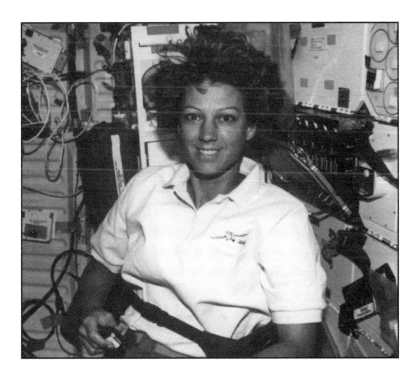

Eileen Collins aboard Columbia *on the mission she commanded. In 2000, Collins received the French Legion of Honor for her outstanding contributions to mankind, in particular this successful STS-93 mission. European Space Agency astronaut Michel Tognini, from France, was a member of her crew.*

Center in Florida. In a storybook ending to a textbook mission, Collins rolled the big glider to a stop just miles from where it had lifted off. Perhaps it wasn't exactly what she had envisioned flying all those summers ago on Harris Hill, but Eileen Collins wasn't complaining. She currently has no plans to leave NASA.

The flight of STS-93 closed a wound that had festered for 36 years. Valentina Tereshkova's 1963 trip into space was hailed as a major step forward for women. It wasn't. Rumors persisted that she had lost her composure. Partly because of this uncertainty, 19 years passed before another woman—Soviet cosmonaut Svetlana Savitskaya—orbited Earth.

Two years later, in July 1984, Savitskaya became the first woman to walk in space. Women were finally making real strides. Already Sally Ride, America's first woman astronaut, had flown in June 1983. The uncertainty vanished even further in October 1984 when astronaut Kathryn Sullivan made America's first space walk by a woman. Interestingly, women gained less attention as they achieved more. Collins herself noticed that her second shuttle flight drew far less media attention than the first. Her command of *Columbia* healed the breach between men and women space travelers for good. "Eventually," Collins had predicted before her historic flight, "having women in these roles won't be news anymore." And no news, she added, would be just fine with her.

140

Astronaut Shannon Wells Lucid (b. 1943) lived aboard
Mir *for 188 days in 1996, setting a record for the*
longest stay in space by an American. She worked out on
a treadmill on Mir *to keep fit. Lucid flew on four*
shuttle missions before her historic stay in space.

In June 1983, Sally
Kristen Ride (b. 1951)
joined four other
astronauts aboard
Challenger *and became*
the first American
woman in space. She
flew a second mission in
1984, then worked at
NASA headquarters in
Washington, D.C.,
until 1987. Ride is a
physics professor at the
University of
California, San Diego.

Glossary of Space Terms

airlock: an airtight chamber, with adjustable air pressure, between places that do not have the same air pressure, as between the interior and exterior of a space capsule

altitude: the height of something above a specific reference level

astronaut: a person specially trained to fly, navigate, or work aboard a spacecraft; from the Greek words for space sailor

axis: a straight line about which an object rotates

booster rocket: a rocket stage that powers a spacecraft during liftoff, often jettisoned (left behind) after the fuel is gone

capsule: a pressurized module for carrying astronauts on space flights

centrifuge: an apparatus in which humans or animals are enclosed and which is revolved to simulate space flight acceleration

command module or CM: the section of an Apollo spacecraft containing the crew's living area and the instruments and equipment they needed. It measured about 11 feet high and 13 feet in diameter and had room for three astronauts.

cosmonaut: an astronaut trained in the Soviet Union or, after 1991, Russia or the Republic of Kazakhstan; from the Greek words for universe sailor

decompress: to relieve of pressure; to bring a person gradually back to normal atmospheric conditions

dock: to join two or more spacecraft in space

g-forces or g's: the force of gravity. Earth's gravity is a g-force of one.

glider: a heavier-than-air aircraft that flies with no engine

gravity: the attraction of the mass of a celestial body, such as Earth, for other bodies. Gravity creates a sense of weight and causes objects to fall.

intercontinental ballistic missile (ICBM): a long-range military rocket armed with a nuclear weapon, designed to make suborbital flights and then reenter the atmosphere. The Atlas and Titan rockets that launched the Mercury and Gemini spacecraft, respectively, were ICBMs adapted for space travel.

launch pad: a fireproof platform used as a base from which spacecraft are launched into space

liftoff: the moment a rocket starts traveling into the sky

liquid-fuel rocket: a rocket propelled by chemical fuels and oxidizers, substances such as liquid oxygen that enable the fuel to burn

lunar: anything relating to the Moon

lunar module or lander or LM: a spacecraft designed to carry astronauts from the Apollo command module to the Moon's surface and back

Lunar Orbit Rendezvous (LOR): the method NASA chose to send astronauts to the Moon, requiring a three-part spacecraft. Pronounced L-O-R. *See also* **command module** and **lunar module**

NASA: National Aeronautics and Space Administration, established October 1, 1958, to direct U.S. exploration of space

observatory: a building or instrument designed to watch astronomical bodies or phenomena such as black holes

orbit: the path of one body as it circles another, such as Earth around the Sun, or a satellite around Earth

orbiter: the piloted section of the space shuttle that travels in space and lands like an airplane

payload bay: the area of the space shuttle, behind the crew compartment and in front of the engines, used to carry cargo. In orbit, double doors in the payload bay can be opened to deploy, or release, cargo.

pitch: motion of a spacecraft in which the nose moves up or down

pressurize: to maintain normal air pressure in an enclosure

rendezvous: the close approach of two spacecraft in orbit that then stay close together, sometimes followed by the docking of the two craft

retrorocket: a rocket engine that fires in the direction the spacecraft is traveling in order to slow the craft down. *See also* **rocket**

rocket: a device that moves usually by burning fuel and expelling the resulting hot gases from one end. The rocket travels in the opposite direction from the escaping gases.

roll: motion of a spacecraft in which it spins along its horizontal axis like a top

satellite: a small celestial body that orbits a larger one, such as the Moon traveling around Earth. An artificial satellite is a man-made object that can orbit Earth, such as a weather satellite.

service module: the section of an Apollo spacecraft that contained the spacecraft's main engine, fuel cells, water, and other supplies

space: the vast region beyond the atmosphere of Earth

space shuttle: a spacecraft made up of an orbiter, two solid rocket boosters, and an external fuel tank. The orbiter is the part that actually travels through space and returns to Earth, gliding to a landing much like an airplane. The boosters are dropped over the Atlantic Ocean after launch, recovered, and reused. The external fuel tank, used only once, contains liquid oxygen and liquid hydrogen propellants for the main engine.

space sickness: temporary dizziness and nausea that sometimes affects people traveling in space

space suit: a protective garment with life-support and communication systems that enable the wearer to survive in space

space walk: any activity by an astronaut or cosmonaut outside the spacecraft or on the surface of the Moon

suborbital: a flight made by a rocket or spacecraft in which the object reaches space, but does not travel fast enough to attain orbit and falls back to Earth in a long curve

thrust: the driving force that pushes a rocket engine forward

weightlessness: the absence of the noticeable effects of gravity

yaw: motion of a spacecraft in which its nose moves sideways

Internet Resources

National Aeronautics and Space Administration sites

http://www.nasa.gov
   NASA's homepage

http://www.nasa.gov/hqpao/women_ac.htm
   NASA site celebrating women's achievements in space
   and aviation

http://nix.nasa.gov
   Browse through a selection of NASA photos

http://lsda.jsc.nasa.gov/apollo/astp.stm
   Apollo-Soyuz Test Project

http://nssdc.gsfc.nasa.gov/planetary/lunar/lunartimeline.html
   Complete lunar exploration timeline

http://www.grc.nasa.gov/WWW/bpp
   Breakthrough propulsion physics page

http://spaceflight.nasa.gov
   Human space-flight page, with information on current
   shuttle flights, space station missions, and photo gallery

http://www.dfrc.nasa.gov
   Dryden Flight Research Center homepage

http://www.lerc.nasa.gov
   Glenn Research Center homepage

http://www.lerc.nasa.gov/WWW/PAO/warp.htm
   Glenn Research Center; discusses warp drive

http://www.jpl.nasa.gov
   Jet Propulsion Lab at California Institute of
   Technology homepage

http://www.jsc.nasa.gov
   Johnson Space Center homepage

http://www.ksc.nasa.gov
 Kennedy Space Center homepage

http://oea.larc.nasa.gov
 Langley Research Center homepage

http://www.msfc.nasa.gov
 Marshall Space Flight Center homepage

http://history.msfc.nasa.gov
 History site of Marshall Space Flight Center

http://www.ssl.msfc.nasa.gov/ssl/pad/solar/skylab.htm
 Marshall Space Flight Center with wealth of
 information on *Skylab*

http://quest.arc.nasa.gov
 NASA educational resources

http://www.hq.nasa.gov
 NASA headquarters

http://www.hq.nasa.gov/office/pao/History/on-line.html
 Lists all NASA histories that are available free online;
 excellent site

National Air and Space Museum sites

http://www.nasm.edu
 NASM homepage

http://www.nasm.edu/apollo
 Information site for Apollo missions

http://www.nasm.edu/nasm/dsh/oralhistory.html
 Oral history project from NASM with a link to its
 catalog of online interviews

Other Recommended Sites

http://howe.iki.rssi.ru/GCTC/gctc_e.htm
 Yuri Gagarin Cosmonauts Training Center, located in
 Star City

http://www.astronauts.org
 Astronaut hall of fame

http://www.edwards.af.mil/about_edwards/index.html
  Edwards Air Force Base homepage

http://www.friends-partners.org/mwade/
  Encyclopedia Astronautica homepage; complete index
  of all astronauts and cosmonauts. Highly
  recommended.

http://www.lifemag.com/Life/space/giantleap/sec3/schirra1.html
  Life magazine article written by Wally Schirra

http://www.lifemag.com/Life/space/starcity/starcity01.html
  Life magazine article about Star City, the cosmonaut
  training facility

http://www.nationalaviation.org
  National Aviation Hall of Fame, biographies

http://www.pbs.org/kcts/astronauts/interact/launch/
launch4.html
  Public Broadcasting System site with links to various
  national space programs

http://www.pbs.org/wgbh/nova/tothemoon
  This is a companion site to NOVA's "To the Moon," a
  two-hour documentary on how astronauts reached the
  Moon. Includes a transcript of the show. (NOVA
  transcripts for the last several years are available free
  online.)

http://www.planetary.org
  The Planetary Society homepage; check out links to
  online exploration resources

http://www.solarviews.com
  Multimedia site about the solar system and the history
  of space exploration

http://www.space.com
  Much information about space, astronomy, etc.,
  including educational pages for students K-12

Bibliography

Books

Armstrong, Neil, Michael Collins, and Edwin E. Aldrin Jr. *First on the Moon*. Written with Gene Farmer and Dora Jane Hamblin. Boston: Little, Brown, 1970.

Baker, David. *The History of Manned Space Flight*. New York: Crown Publishers, 1981.

Bond, Peter. *Heroes in Space: From Gagarin to Challenger*. New York: Basil Blackwell, 1987.

Breuer, William B. *Race to the Moon: America's Duel with the Soviets*. Westport, Conn.: Praeger Publishers, 1993.

Brooks, Courtney G., James M. Grimwood, and Loyd S. Swenson Jr. *Chariots for Apollo: A History of Manned Lunar Spacecraft*. The NASA History Series: NASA SP-4205. Washington, D.C.: NASA, 1979.

Cassutt, Michael. *Who's Who in Space: The International Space Year Edition*. New York: Macmillan, 1993.

Clark, Phillip. *The Soviet Manned Space Program*. New York: Orion Books, 1988.

Cooper, Henry S. F., Jr. *Before Lift-off: The Making of a Space Shuttle Crew*. Baltimore: Johns Hopkins University Press, 1987.

Dethloff, Henry C. *Suddenly, Tomorrow Came . . . : A History of the Johnson Space Center*. The NASA History Series: NASA SP-4307. Houston: NASA, 1993.

Ezell, Edward Clinton, and Linda Neuman Ezell. *The Partnership: A History of the Apollo-Soyuz Test Project*. Washington, D.C.: NASA, 1978.

Gagarin, Yuri, and Vladimir Lebedev. *Survival in Space*. New York: Praeger Publishers, 1969.

Goldstein, Stanley H. *Reaching for the Stars: The Story of Astronaut Training and the Lunar Landing*. New York: Praeger Publishers, 1987.

Hacker, Barton C., and Charles C. Alexander. *On the Shoulders of Titans: A History of Project Gemini*. The NASA History Series: NASA SP-4203. Washington, D.C.: NASA, 1977.

Hansen, James R. *Spaceflight Revolution: NASA Langley Research Center from Sputnik to Apollo*. The NASA History Series: NASA SP-4308. Washington, D.C.: NASA, 1995.

Information Summaries: Astronaut Fact Book. NP-1998-07-008JSC. NASA online publication: http://www.hq.nasa.gov/office/pao/History/nautfb.pdf.

Lewis, Richard S. *The Voyages of Columbia: The First True Spaceship*. New York: Columbia University Press, 1984.

Logsdon, John M. *The Decision to Go to the Moon*. Cambridge, Mass.: MIT Press, 1970.

Murray, Charles, and Catherine Bly Cox. *Apollo: The Race to the Moon*. New York: Simon and Schuster, 1989.

Neufeld, Michael J. *The Rocket and the Reich*. Cambridge, Mass.: Harvard University Press, 1995.

Newkirk, Dennis. *Almanac of Soviet Manned Space Flight*. Houston: Gulf Publishing, 1990.

Oberg, James E. *The New Race For Space*. Harrisburg, Penn.: Stackpole Books, 1984.

————. *Red Star in Orbit*. New York: Random House, 1981.

———. *Uncovering Soviet Disasters*. New York: Random House, 1988.

Ordway, Frederick Ira, III, and Mitchell R. Sharpe. *The Rocket Team*. New York: Crowell, 1979.

Popovich, Pavel, ed. *Orbits of Peace and Progress*. Moscow: Mir Publishers, 1988.

Results of the Third U.S. Manned Orbital Space Flight October 3, 1962. (Wally Schirra's flight.) Washington, D.C.: NASA, 1962.

Riabchikov, Evgeny. *Russians in Space*. Garden City, N.Y.: Doubleday, 1971.

Schefter, James. *The Race: The Uncensored Story of How America Beat Russia to the Moon*. New York: Doubleday, 1999.

Schirra, Walter M., Jr., and Richard N. Billings. *Schirra's Space*. Boston: Quinlan Press, 1988.

Segel, Thomas. *Men in Space*. Boulder, Colo.: Paladin Press, 1975.

Sharpe, Mitchell R. *"It is I, Sea Gull:" Valentina Tereshkova, First Woman in Space*. New York: Crowell, 1975.

———. *Yuri Gagarin: First Man in Space*. Huntsville, Ala.: Strode Publishers, 1969.

Shepard, Alan, and Deke Slayton. *Moon Shot: The Inside Story of America's Race to the Moon*. Atlanta: Turner Publishing, 1994.

Slayton, Donald K. "Deke," and Michael Cassutt. *Deke! U.S. Manned Space: From Mercury to the Shuttle*. New York: Tom Doherty, 1994.

Swenson, Loyd S., Jr.; James M. Grimwood; and Charles C. Alexander. *This New Ocean: A History of Project Mercury*. The NASA History Series: NASA SP-4201. Washington, D.C.: NASA, 1989.

Welch, Rosanne. *Encyclopedia of Women in Aviation and Space*. Santa Barbara, Calif.: ABC-CLIO, 1998.

Westman, Paul. *John Young: Space Shuttle Commander*. Minneapolis: Dillon Press, 1981.

Zheleznyakov, Aleksandr. "Aleksej Arkhipovich Leonov," compiled by the author from his personal archive and his book *Soviet Space Explorations: Chronology of Accidents and Catastrophes*. Translated by Alex Greenberg.

Newspapers/Periodicals

Dickey, Beth. "After Hiccup at Liftoff, Shuttle Puts Telescope Into Space." *The New York Times*, July 24, 1999.

———. "Woman's Work: Space Commander." *The New York Times*, July 24, 1999.

"Lift-off to a New Space Era." *Life*, April 2, 1965.

"Moscow Welcomes the Cosmonauts." *Life*, April 2, 1965.

Video Documentaries

"The Idea That Nobody Wanted." NASA Langley Research Center: Video Applications Group.

"To The Moon." (Public Broadcasting System/NOVA) NASA Langley Research Center: Video Applications Group.

Index

140, 141; creation of, 13, 76, 77, 93; Moon mission planned by, 97, 114; and shuttle program, 118, 120-121, 127, 136; in space race, 17, 57, 76; training of astronauts by, 78, 93, 110, 134

Nikolayev, Andrian Grigoryevich, 50, 51

Nikolayev, Yelena, 50

Nixon, Richard, 68

North Ray Crater, 117

Oberth, Hermann, 9

Orion, 116, 117

Paresev, 89

Patterson, Frank, 132

pitch, 81

Project High Jump, 109-110

propellants, 7, 8, 122

Redstone rocket, 78

rendezvous (of spacecraft), 71, 87, 118; attempted by Soviets, 16, 45-46; first, 17, 70, 73, 83-84, 113; during Gemini missions, 57, 83, 84, 93, 94, 95, 111; importance of, in space program, 15, 53, 81-82, 97, 110; of shuttle, 19, 136

Ride, Sally, 18, 140, 141

rockets: Agena, 95, 96, 113; GIRD-X, 10; history of, 8-11; liquid-fuel, 6, 7-8, 10, 25; Redstone, 78; retro,

32, 33, 65; Saturn 5, 98, 100, 118, 119; solid-propellant booster, 122, 123, 128; Titan, 72, 73, 82, 112; V-2, 8-9, 108

Salyut, 18, 66, 67

satellite, 11, 12, 26, 27, 38, 40, 42, 54, 76, 118, 127

Saturn 5 rocket, 98, 100, 118, 119

Savitskaya, Svetlana, 18, 140

Schirra, Florence Shillito Leach, (mother), 73

Schirra, Josephine Fraser (wife), 86

Schirra, Suzanne Karen (daughter), 86

Schirra, Walter "Wally" Marty, Jr., 14; and aborted launch of *Gemini 6*, 71-73, 82; *Apollo* 7 flight of, 86; astronaut training of, 77-78; early years of, 73-74; and first rendezvous, 17, 70, 71, 83, 94, 113; Gemini missions of, 72, 82-84; Mercury missions of, 73, 80-81; as pilot, 70, 71, 74-75, 85, 87, 133; selection of, for Mercury program, 76-77

Schirra, Walter Marty, Sr. (father), 73

Schirra, Walter Marty, III (son), 86

Scott, David R., 94, 95, 96, 97, 113

Vanguard, 42
Voskhod: program, 57; spacecraft, 54, 55, 57, 58-59, 61, 64, 65, 66
Voskhod 1, 54, 57
Voskhod 2, 54, 57, 58-59, 60, 61, 64, 65, 66
Vostok: cosmonauts of, 13-14; program, 53, 56, 57, 58; spacecraft, 14, 15-16, 19, 29-30, 45, 46, 53, 56, 57, 58. *See also* individual missions
Vostok 1, 14-15, 22, 23, 30-31, 32, 33, 42
Vostok 2, 41
Vostok 5, 45, 46
Vostok 6, 16, 45, 46, 48, 51
V-2 rocket, 8-9, 108

weightlessness, 13, 29, 33, 37, 41, 45, 48, 53, 59, 78, 134, 135
White, Edward H., II, 61, 84, 85, 113, 114
Winkler, Johannes, 8
Women's Air Force Service Pilots (WASP), 129, 130, 131
World War I, 73
World War II, 9, 24, 39, 55, 74, 77, 108, 129, 130, 131
Wright, Orville, 132
Wright, Wilbur, 132

X-15 rocket plane, 89, 92-93
X-20, 89

yaw, 81
Yegorov, Boris, 55
Young, Barbara (wife), 110
Young, Hugh (father), 108
Young, John Watts, 57, 107; as administrator at Johnson Space Center, 125; Apollo missions of, 98, 106, 115-117, 118; astronaut training of, 110-111; early years of, 108-109; firsts of, 106, 110, 113, 118, 119; Gemini missions of, 57, 106, 111, 112, 113, 118; as pilot, 109, 110, 133; shuttle flights of, 17, 108, 118-119, 122-124
Young, John Watts, Jr. (son), 110
Young, Sandra (daughter), 110
Young Communist League, 40
Youngs, Pat, 132

ABOUT THE AUTHOR

JASON RICHIE is the author of several titles from The Oliver Press, including *Secretaries of State: Making Foreign Policy*; *Secretaries of War, Navy, and Defense: Ensuring National Security*; *Space Flight: Crossing the Last Frontier*; and *Weapons: Designing the Tools of War*. A former noncommissioned officer in the U.S. Army, Richie graduated *summa cum laude* from the University of Minnesota with a degree in American history. He lives in Houston, Texas, with his wife, Diana, and son, James.

Photo Credits